Weighing up the Evidence

TIMELINE:

South Africa

Sarah Harris

Dryad Press Limited London

Contents

This book is dedicated
to the 4,000 or more children
who are detained, without trial,
in prisons
in South Africa

First published 1988

Typeset by Tek-Art Ltd, Kent
and printed and bound in Great Britain by
Richard Clay Ltd,
Chichester, Sussex
for the Publishers
Dryad Press Limited,
8 Cavendish Square,
London W1M 0AJ

ISBN 0 8521 9724 1

ACKNOWLEDGMENTS

The author and publishers thank the following for their kind permission to reproduce copyright illustrations: Illustrated London News Picture Library, page 23; International Defence and Aid Fund for Southern Africa, pages 8, 9, 14, 17, 18, 28, 32, 33, 41, 52, 55; Popperfoto, pages 12, 47. The maps on pages 6, 12, 24 and 38 are by R.F. Brien. The author would like to thank Nick Harris, Ian Linden, Kate Morse, John Paterson and Maggie Paterson for help in the preparation of this book.

Front cover: *top*, troops in the township of Tsakwe, East Rand (International Defence and Aid Fund for Southern Africa); *bottom left*, Khoi-Khoi building their huts on the Cape frontier (International Defence and Aid Fund for Southern Africa); *bottom right*, killing cattle on the Rodden river (BBC Hulton Picture Library).

Introduction

On 12 June 1986 the South African government declared a State of Emergency throughout its country, imposed severe reporting restrictions on the press (both domestic and foreign) and imprisoned, without trial or charge, a large but indeterminate number of its people, the vast majority of whom were black and therefore not citizens of their own state.

The declaration occurred as this book began to be written and thus served to emphasize the difficulties of writing a history book that attempts to trace the historical development of this unique African state and its system of Apartheid. South Africa is in a state of turmoil; the contradictions built in to its social organization are unresolved. The world unites to condemn Apartheid but is divided about whether to act against the South African government. In such a context, to write a book that attempts to describe and analyse, briefly and simply, the processes by which the present situation came about is a hard task.

This book is written by an author who regards Apartheid as morally indefensible. But the author also regards Apartheid and the present situation in South Africa as historically explicable and understandable. To explain and understand events and historical development is not to justify them morally. For example, we can explain and understand how the Nazi Party came to power in Germany in 1933, and what the forces and attitudes and fears were that were operating in German society at that time, that enabled the genocide of the Jews and gypsies and the persecution of Christians, socialists and other dissenters to take place. Explaining what happened does not justify it, as there is nothing inevitable about history.

When faced with an emotive and moral problem in history, one of the most important skills an historian has to call upon is the skill of empathy. This means attempting to understand all the forces such as religion, morality, economic position, social attitudes, fear, understanding, that come together to influence human behaviour and affect historical events. We must be careful not to ascribe to other peoples in other circumstances our own view of things. We must search for insights into their view. Otherwise their behaviour becomes inexplicable and the events in which they participated beyond understanding.

This book traces the development of South Africa from before the Europeans arrived until 1983 and the formation of the United Democratic Front. It uses original source material and other evidence to illustrate the forces at work in South Africa that have led to the present crisis, and it sets questions and tasks that are designed to help you understand and analyse the changes and developments that are taking place. The book is organized chronologically, but is not an exhaustive study of South Africa's history. Many important events are not mentioned and many important leaders are not described. It is hoped that the themes in the book will encourage you to search out other information about South Africa, to develop further your understanding of this most complicated and difficult country.

Many studies of South Africa available to young people describe its history almost uniquely from the point of view of Britain and its imperial past. Some attempt is made in this book to present a more balanced picture. The history of the black people in South Africa is not the same as the history of the Afrikaners or of the British. In much of this book the histories of black and white South Africans are separated out to show that more clearly. Each chapter also looks at the interaction between black and white history. It might help to explain this point by giving an example nearer to home.

Most "British" history we study is, in fact, English history – especially before the nineteenth century. It is also mostly English "male" history. The histories of Wales and Scotland – their societies, economies, philosophies – and the history of women – their achievements, attitudes and roles – are discounted. This is partly because a great deal of history is about a study of power, and English power and male power not only used to control but also still control our lives. But to understand the present role and attitudes of women in our society, or to understand the emergence of nationalism or the different voting patterns of communities in Wales and Scotland today, we must look at the different histories of women and minority communities in British society.

In South Africa, power is currently held by the minority group of whites. This power is being challenged by the majority population of black and coloured people. Perhaps, if that challenge were not taking place, we could ignore the people and their history, as we ignore great chunks of our own; but we cannot hope to understand South Africa today without looking at the unique experience of black people and at their past.

Black people in South Africa are also trying to discover and recapture their past. In all South African schools the history syllabuses and the history books give no account of black history. Increasingly, black South Africans see a part of their struggle as "a struggle of memory against forgetting".

At the end of this book there is an epilogue which outlines but does not analyse some of the events that have taken place in South Africa since 1983. The Timeline puts the history of South Africa in a British, world and wider African context; and the Book List and Sources section will help you find material through which you can explore the issues further. The Glossary lists specialist words whose meaning you need to know.

One of the main purposes in studying history is to understand the problems and difficulties people face, the strategies they employ in attempting to overcome them, and the forces at work in society which affect both their choices and the outcomes. These are not simple ideas to think about, but trying to do so should inform *our* choices and understanding. South Africa may seem very far away in distance and very different in the problems it faces, but the struggle of its black people can illuminate our understanding of the position of black and oppressed people all over the world; and the fears of the white South Africans have much in common with the fears of any group facing a challenge to its monopoly of power. These are questions it is worth reflecting on.

The Southern Tip of Africa, to 1867

THE PROBLEMS FACING HISTORIANS

An eighteenth-century philosopher called George Berkeley expounded the view that any object existed only at the moment when it was perceived. He used as an example a tree growing in the quadrangle of his college, which, he argued, existed only when it was seen as existing by a mind. A populist version of this theory was subsequently memorably rendered in two limericks:

There was once a man who said 'God
Must think it exceedingly odd
   If he finds that this tree
   Continues to be
When there's no one about in the Quad.'

(*Source:* "Limerick on Idealism", attributed to Langford Reed, *The Limerick Book*, R.A. Knox , 1888-1957)

The reply went:

Dear Sir, your astonishment's odd:
I am always about in the Quad.
   And that's why the tree
   Will continue to be,
Since observed by Yours Faithfully, God.

(*Source:* Reply to "Limerick on Idealism", Anon.)

This is not quite such an irrelevant start to a history book on South Africa as it may appear. For years, historians have confined themselves almost exclusively to the study of the white community, which did not obtain a permanent foothold at the Cape until the second half of the seventeenth century. They have treated very briefly, if at all, the history of the African peoples before they were subjected to white over-rule, and even then they have seen it only from the point of view of how Africans responded to contact from Europeans. Like the tree in the quad, the Africans have been thought to exist only when perceived and acted upon by the European mind.

There are, of course, technical difficulties in studying the history of peoples before they produced written records of their own. But the failure to study systematically the black history of Southern Africa cannot be explained by a dearth of data. Enormous amounts of relevant source material are available in Europe, including books and articles by white travellers, missionaries and traders, specialized articles by archeologists, linguists and anthropologists, and compilations of the oral traditions of African societies. Much of this material needs to be carefully handled. The accounts abound with the prejudices, preconceived ideas and convictions of their authors and compilers. But the fact that a particular source may be biased, or unreliable, or written for another purpose, does not make it any the less useful for an historian, provided that it is approached with understanding and rigour, checked for inconsistencies within itself and matched against other materials.

Since the end of colonial rule in Africa and the creation of independent African states, and with the growth of black consciousness in both Africa and the U.S.A., a great deal of work has begun to be done to fill in the gaps in our knowledge and improve our understanding of development and change in non-white African societies. Perhaps more importantly, black South Africans themselves are now at work recapturing their own history from white control.

SOUTH AFRICAN PEOPLES

The Bantu-speaking peoples:

This group includes the Tswana, the Sotho, the Venda, the Pedi, the Thonga and the Nguni peoples. These peoples expanded south and south-east from Zimbabwe and the Northern Transvaal from probably about the ninth century onwards, and possibly much earlier. They knew how to make iron implements, and the communities living inland also developed a considerable technology in stone. The Sotho and Tswana lived in the area west of the Drakensburg mountains and were pastoralists, i.e. they herded cattle. They lived in large settlements (often of more then 10,000 people),

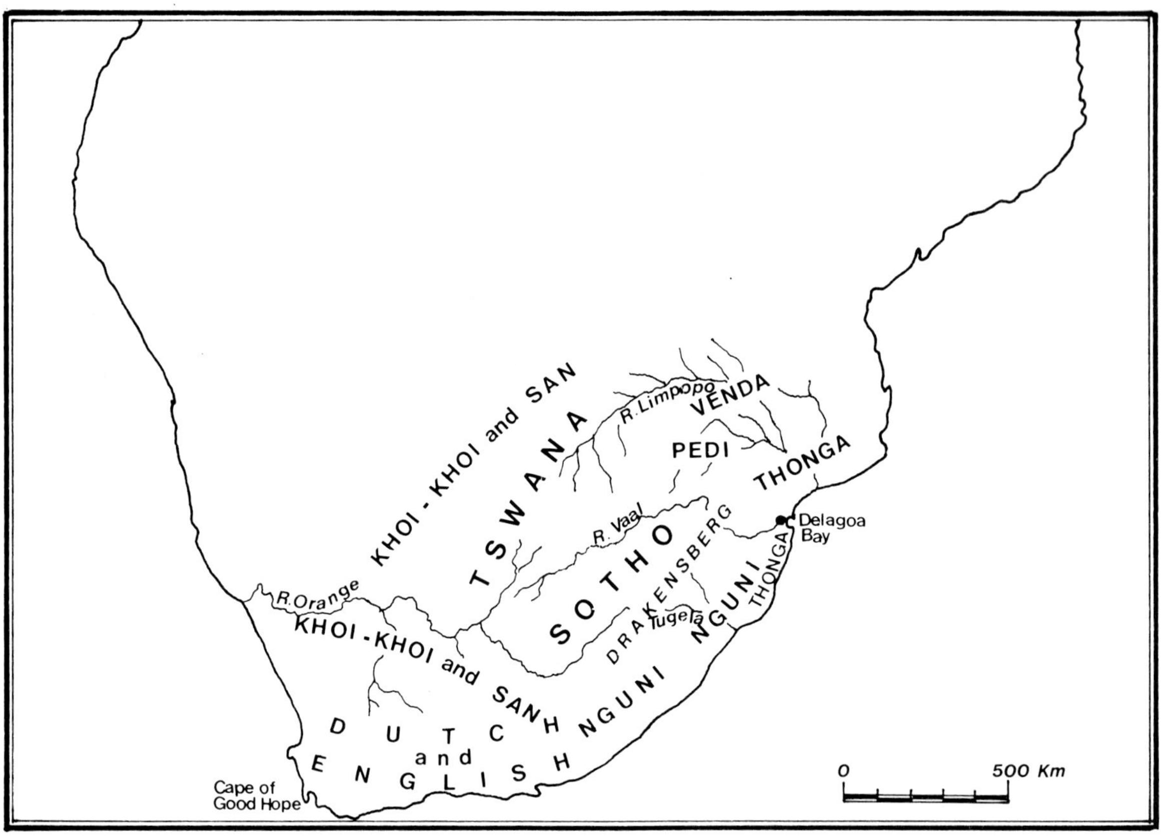

Language groups in Southern Africa south of the Limpopo, at the beginning of the nineteenth century.

which were, in effect, towns. In 1800 the Tswana towns were probably the largest in Southern Africa. Living in urban communities enables political centralization to take place and economic specialization to occur. Thus the Tswana and Sotho Chiefs exercised considerable authority over their settlements, and large numbers of workers were occupied in metal and stone crafts, while living off the easily distributable surplus of those engaged in food production.

To the east of the Drakensburg mountains, in the narrow coastal strip, lived the Nguni and Thonga peoples. The Thonga had the closest contact with the outside world. Since the sixteenth century they had engaged in trade with the Portuguese, and before that they may well have been trading with the Arabs. Alone of the Southern African peoples they became involved in the Slave Trade, providing war-captives to the Portuguese. The coastal area they populated was not suitable for cattle rearing and they depended on trade for their livelihood.

To the south of the Thonga were the Nguni peoples. They were cattle keepers and cultivators. Their political units were collections of clans, and among each of these the Chief's clan was pre-eminent. However, his authority was not arbitrary and it was within the power of the people to break up a community and transer their allegiance to a new leader. The land the Nguni occupied provided a comfortable existence and they also engaged in some trade with the Portuguese to the north, around Delagoa Bay. So pleasant and settled were the Nguni communities that many white shipwrecked sailors chose to stay and live among them, and travellers commented favourably on their lack of crime and poverty.

Journal of a Voyage in 1798 to Da Lagoa Bay:

. . . Divorces are not in fashion at Da Lagoa for the men are all faithful, and the women, though nearly naked, virtuous. . .

They are a very honest set of people, but great beggars . . . this they have learnt, I imagine, from the Portuguese. . .

All the labour and work is done by the women. . . . In going to any of their villages, you find men mostly sitting in circles round a fire, smoking tobacco and bang, dressing their hair, making bird-cages, or some other trivial occupation, while the women were employed in beating Indian corn, maize, rice, and other necessary occupations. . .

You get a variety of very fine fish, all of a most excellent quality, much superior to any I have seen in India: they are wholesome good food, and cost a mere trifle. Mullet, carp, conger eels . . . sun-fish, skate, shrimps, prawns, crabs, oysters, cockles etc. are the different sorts. . .

The climate of Da Lagoa I think healthy; we all found it so. . .

The whole face of the country is truly pleasant. From the Red Head you has a fine a prospect as I ever saw.

(*Source: Journal of a Voyage . . . in the Year 1798*, William White, Captain, 73rd Highland Regiment of Foot)

Why do you think Captain White found the virtuousness of the people and the fact that women did the work remarkable?

The earlier inhabitants:

Drawings of Khoi-Khoi and San people made by Europeans visiting the Cape in the eighteenth century. Does the fact that Europeans drew the pictures make them less useful or less reliable as evidence?

In the arid western area of the peninsula lived the Khoi-Khoi and the San. They were the original inhabitants of the southern tip of Africa and had been pushed west and south by the expansion of the Bantu peoples (see page 6). They shared a Stone Age technology and a language characterized by clicks, but whereas the Khoi-Khoi were cattle herders, the San were hunters and gatherers. There had been close contact between the Khoi-Khoi and the southernmost Nguni (the Xhosa) for centuries. Some of the clicks had been absorbed into the Xhosa language and many Khoi-Khoi lived under the protection of their more powerful neighbours. The Khoi-Khoi also depended on the Xhosa for the iron they needed and, in exchange, traded with them in items unobtainable to the east, such as feathers and ivory.

THE MFECANE – THE CRUSHING OF PEOPLES

Probably the most significant factor of black history in the early nineteenth century was the political transformation of the northern Nguni. The period is described by Nguni speakers as the Mfecane, and by Sotho speakers as the Difaqane, but both words mean "the crushing of peoples". This conveys how dramatically the Southern African communities were affected.

Before, disagreements and disputes among the Nguni peoples living in the rich areas between the Drakensburg and the sea had been solved by small groups breaking away and forming new political units. But towards the end of the eighteenth century this peaceful way of solving disputes came to an end. Quite what were the sufficient causes for this change is almost impossible to determine. Almost certainly, the growth of population and the resultant pressure on land contributed to it. It is probable that increased trade with Delagoa Bay and the desire of Chiefs to concentrate this trade in their own hands helped. To some extent, the concentration of political control into the hands of powerful individuals, and the tightening-up of communities, can be seen happening all over Africa at this time. Among the northern Nguni the change was so swift and dramatic that it deserves the name of revolution. It distorted and altered the way change was happening elsewhere. As a result, earlier, gentler movements towards statehood become less significant.

Flight:

Even to European observers something dramatic and different was obviously taking place.

> Ever since our arrival at Delagoa, we had daily received intelligence from the panic-struck natives of the depredations committing among them by the Oratontahs . . . which in their language signifies a robber. Their [the Oratontahs'] country was situated at a considerable distance to the southward, and they had left it, to the number of many hundreds, some time before. . .
>
> Whether they commenced their depredations about Delagoa before 1821 I could not learn, but at that period they certainly carried devastation and terror wherever they appeared.
>
> (*Source:* Thomas Boteler, *Narrative of a Voyage of Discovery, 1822*, Vol. I, published 1835)

THE CREATION OF THE ZULU STATE

In the 1790s Dingiswayo emerged as Chief of the Mthethwa, a Nguni tribe living in the south of the northern Nguni area. By the time of his death in 1818 he had transformed the political and military organization of his people and absorbed into the tribe a number of smaller and less well-organized communities, including the Zulu community. Dingiswayo was succeeded by Shaka, a Zulu who he had promoted to Chief of the Zulu client community. Shaka transformed the military tactics of the newly militarized state and further concentrated political power in his own hands by a series of personal appointments. By 1828 a single political unit had been forged in an area, which we can properly call a nation-state, spreading north to Delagoa Bay and south to Natal. The Zulu dialect of Nguni had become standard throughout the country and the traditions of the Zulu people became the traditions of all its citizens. Young people from all the various Nguni groups could share a common pride in belonging to a most powerful state. They thought of themselves as Ama-Zulu, part of the great Zulu family.

In 1828 Shaka was assassinated. However, by then, the Zulu nation, as it was now called, was an unbeatable military machine as far as Bantu technology ws concerned. Those groups that resisted being absorbed into the new state were forced south and north as refugees. Besieged states were forced into similar centralized organizations in order to protect themselves, and the Zulu had earned a reputation as formidable and warlike opponents. Among African societies they had no friends.

Zulu military organization, c. 1830:

The king also distinguished his regiments by giving them shields differently coloured. The great warriors have white shields with one or two black spots; the young warriors have all black shields; the middle warriors, or those that have wives, form distinct regiments, and are called Umfaudas (inferiors), have red shields.

All the regiments form three armies, and have a portion of each of three distinctions in each army. The first army is called 'Umbalabale, or Invincibles', the second 'Umboolalio, or the slaughterers', and the third 'Toogooso, or the hide-aways'.

(*Source:* Nathaniel Isaacs, *Travels and Adventures in Eastern Africa*, London, 1836)

What do you think was the purpose of identifying the troops with different shields? Do other armies have a comparable practice?

WHITE SETTLEMENT IN SOUTHERN AFRICA FROM 1652

In 1652 the Dutch East India Company decided to establish a refreshment station, protected by a small garrison, at the Cape of Good Hope. This was for their ships on the long trade journey from Holland to the Dutch East Indies. In 1657 the first Dutch settlers came to the Cape and began to make something of a living by provisioning the garrison and the port and keeping cattle in the hinterland. In 1658 the settlers introduced slaves to the colony from the Indies and West Indies, since they found the Khoi-Khoi and particularly the San "inefficient" as unwaged labourers.

Use an atlas to understand the value of the Cape to the Dutch and the British.

The Cape was in a critical strategic position on the route from Europe to the Indies, and this led to its occupation by the English in 1795, during the wars with France. Although they handed it back briefly to the Dutch, the English returned in 1806 and established a permanent occupation.

The Dutch settlers resented the rigour with which the English administered the Cape. The English administration regarded its own interests as paramount. The importance of the Cape was its position on the sea-routes which England controlled. The English had no interest in moving inland. To do so would involve unnecessary and expensive conflict with the Xhosa. As a result, frontier relations with the Xhosa were dictated by these strategic and financial interests, and the interests of the Dutch farmers, who *did* want more land, were not considered. The English insisted that all free men were equal before the law, whatever their colour – though this did not, of course, mean that non-whites were regarded as socially or economically equal. In 1833 an Act of the British Parliament emancipated the slaves.

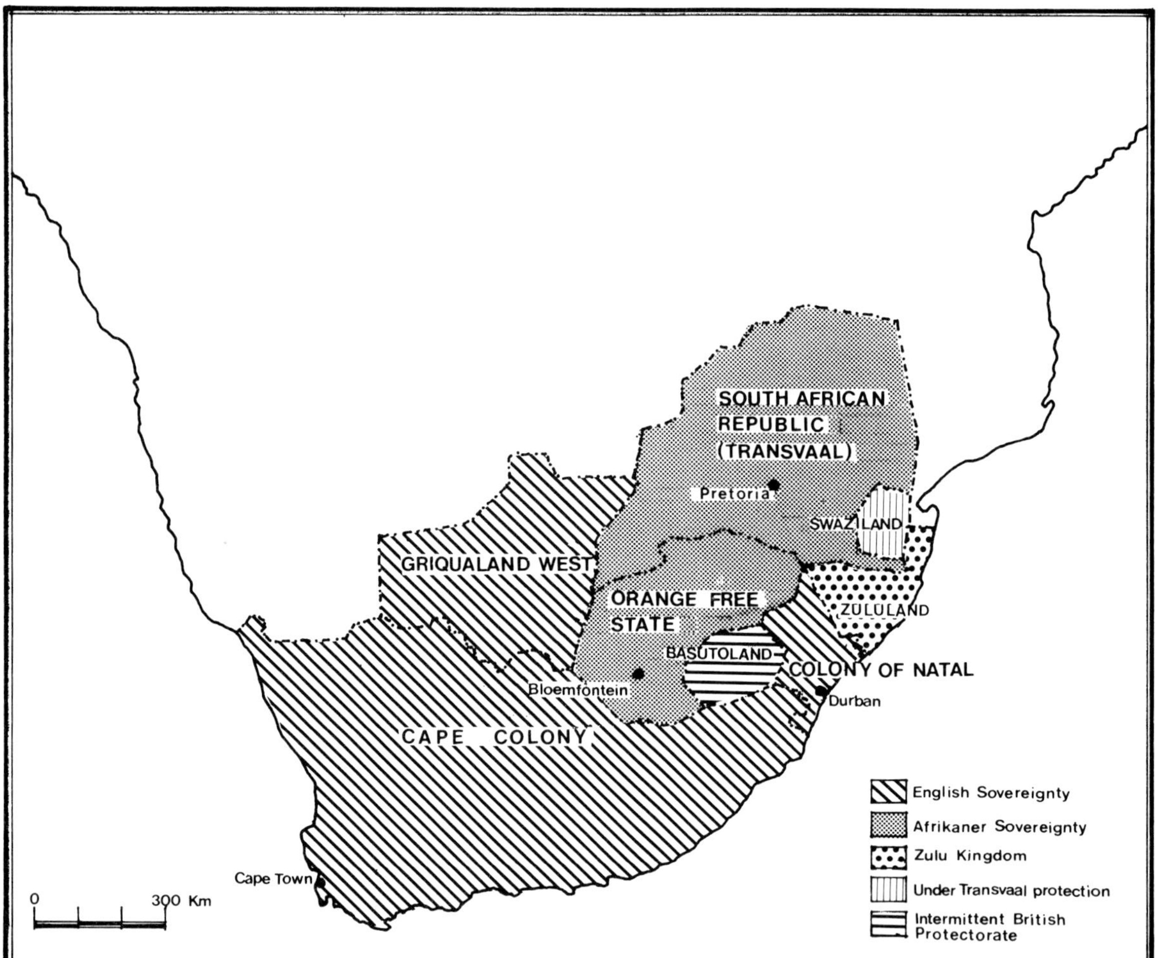
SOUTH AFRICAN REPUBLIC (TRANSVAAL)
Pretoria
SWAZILAND
GRIQUALAND WEST
ORANGE FREE STATE
ZULULAND
BASUTOLAND
COLONY OF NATAL
Bloemfontein
Durban
CAPE COLONY
Cape Town
0
300 Km
English Sovereignty
Afrikaner Sovereignty
Zulu Kingdom
Under Transvaal protection
Intermittent British Protectorate

THE GREAT TREK

The result of these policies was a growing resentment among the Dutch settlers. In 1836, large groups of them began to leave the colony, moving inland to escape English rule. This was called the Great Trek and occupies a central place in the consciousness of the South African Afrikaner peoples, as the descendants of the Dutch settlers came to be known. One of their leaders, Piet Retief, explained the reasons for their leaving in a document published in the *Grahamstown Journal*.

The Grahamstown Manifesto:

. . . we record the following summary of our motives for taking so important a step. . .

1. We despair of saving the colony from those evils which threaten it by the turbulent and dishonest conduct of vagrants. . .
2. We complain of the severe losses which we have been forced to sustain by the emancipation of our slaves. . .
3. We complain of the continual system of plunder which we have ever endured from the Caffres and other coloured classes. . .
4. We complain of the unjustifiable odium which has been cast upon us . . . under the cloak of religion . . . and we can foresee, as the result of this prejudice, nothing but the total ruin of our country.
5. We are resolved . . . that we will uphold the just principles of liberty . . . but it is our determination to maintain such regulations as may suppress crime and preserve proper relations between master and servant. . .

9. We quit this colony, under the full assurance that the English government has nothing more to require of us, and will allow us to govern ourselves without its interference in future. . .

(*Source: Grahamstown Manifesto*, February 1837)

◀ *A Boer wagon leaving Cape Town at the time of the Great Trek. The ox-wagon came to symbolize the spirit and determination of the Great Trek.*

◀ *South Africa in 1854. By 1854 the English presence in the Cape had moved further east and north and a new colony had been established around Durban, called Natal. The trekkers had first tried to settle here, but finding the English still too powerful they had moved north to found two new countries, the Orange Free State and the South African Republic. Three distinct black South African communities existed too: the Zulu kingdom, the kingdom of the Lesotho people (called Basutoland by the English) and the kingdom of the Ngwane people, or Swazi people, as they called themselves in honour of their King Mswati. The Zulu were the chief threat to the Swazi people, who formed an alliance with the Transvaal to protect themselves. For the Lesotho the chief threat came from the Orange Free State, and they looked to England to defend them.*

His sister later added her own explanation for the Trek:

And yet it is not their [the slaves'] freedom that drives us to such lengths, as their being placed on an equal footing with Christians, contrary to the laws of God and the natural distinction of race and religion, so that it was intolerable for any decent Christian to bow down beneath such a yoke; wherefore we rather withdrew in order to preserve our doctrines in purity.

(*Source:* Anna Steenkamp, quoted in *The White Tribe of Africa*, David Harrison, BBC Publications, 1981)

Find out why other groups of people have left their homes to make a new life somewhere else. What reasons did they have for going? Do they have anything in comon with the trekkers? (Some examples to help you are the Pilgrim Fathers and Jewish families moving to Israel.)

THE INTERACTION BETWEEN BLACK AND WHITE SOUTH AFRICANS

Within the colony:

The Khoi-Khoi strongly insisted that we had been appropriating more and more of their land, which had been theirs all these centuries, and on which they had been accustomed to let their cattle graze, etc. They asked if they would be allowed to do such a thing supposing they went to Holland and they added: It would be of little consequence if you people stayed here in the fort, but you come right into the interior and select the best land for yourselves. . .

(*Source:* from the diary of Jan Van Riebeeck, leader of the expedition which in 1652 occupied the Cape)

Dutch settlers at the Cape, in the eighteenth century.

What does the picture tell you about the relationship between white settlers and the indigenous population?

The demand for labour:

[Not much use could be made of] labourers found in the colony, such as Europeans, Hottentots . . . and Fingoes, a few of whom might be picked up about the towns for about 2s 6d per diem, including rations. These would be the best labourers, but cannot always be depended upon, as all of those classes who would accept of employment on the roads are almost sure to be drunkards. [On the other hand] numbers of so called Mantatees [Sotho] are in the habit of entering the N.E. borders of the colony in small parties looking for employment. . . . As they are very steady men I would prefer them to any others, provided they could be obtained in sufficient numbers. . . . They would not cost more than a shilling to fifteen pence a day including rations. . .

(*Source:* Report of an English Inspector of Roads, Grahamstown, 20 November 1856)

Why does the Inspector of Roads prefer the Sotho as labourers to black people already living in the colony?

Diplomatic relations:

Some African communities managed to maintain their independence from direct white control. One such country was Basutoland (now Lesotho), which continued to sustain a fragile formal independence in the face of formidable difficulties.

In 1867 the Ba Sotho (Basuto) king, Moshoeshoe, wrote to the President of the Orange Free State which was threatening another territorial war:

I beg to know what is the cause of this year's war. Last year it was through the wish to enlarge your country. This year it seems that it is caused by your wish to exterminate the Basutos. . .

Last year we made peace with you. I gave you 5,000 head of cattle, but I have not given this country away, it belongs not to me, as you know yourself very well that every country in the world does belong to the people which dwells in it.

If I remove the Basutos, I have nowhere where I can establish them. . . . I cannot consent to buy the lives of my people with the country belonging to them. . .

Now I trust that you will consider well all the matters spoken of in this letter, because I also have been ordered by the government of this country to write as I have done.

(*Source:* King Moshoeshoe to the President of the Orange Free State, 9 July 1867)

ON REFLECTION:

"You know very well that every country in the world does belong to the people which dwells in it."

Can you say to whom Southern Africa "belonged" in 1867?

The Mineral Revolution to Union: South Africa, 1867-1910

On the eve of the mineral revolution in South Africa there existed something of a balance of power between black and white states. If anything, it was likely that, with the passage of time, the black states and the black peasantry living within large areas of the white territories would reassert black dominance in the area. The reasons for this are both political and economic.

The most powerful interest in the area was undoubtedly British. But, at this stage, British policy was motivated mainly by strategic interests and a refusal to allow the colonies to become a financial drain. As a result, although Britain would marginally prefer to ally with white interests, in cases where these conflicted with its own it was more than willing to draw black states into a defensive alliance; hence Britain's support for and protection of Basutoland.

The black states, particularly that of the Zulu, were wealthy, economically viable units, able to support their populations and produce goods for export. In contrast, the white settler states of the interior were bankrupt, their economies inefficient. Trying to support a European-style government and lifestyle without European resources, they became increasingly dependent on the more efficient African farmers. In the Natal, white colonists could not afford to pay sufficiently high wages to attract Africans away from their own productive peasant holdings. Importing Indian labour, which offered a short-term solution to the problem, revealed further economic weaknesses as the immigrants moved off the land and set up businesses in competition with the whites and proved more efficient. The exception to black economic superiority was the area of dense white settlement around the Cape. But even here, though farming was productive, the Cape could not finance any further expansion and the imperial government would not support such adventures.

The discovery of diamonds at the confluence of the Orange and Vaal rivers in 1867 changed all this. In 1870 more diamonds were discovered at Kimberley, and in 1886 gold was found at Witwatersrand in the Transvaal. As a result, the British wanted to control the area; the Afrikaner states now had the promise of enough money to run their countries as they wanted to; and the trading and manufacturing industries of the Cape had the prospect of supplying the great new mining areas which would be built. Black interests and rights were of no account. Britain had no title to the area where diamonds were found, but because it was the strongest power, and because its citizens had the best access to money and the technology needed for extracting the diamonds in bulk, Britain took control and British companies built the mines.

THE MINERAL REVOLUTION AND BLACK SOCIETIES

The discovery of the mineral resources set up a demand above all else for labour. Above all else the labour had to be cheap. For many years, areas of the Eastern Cape and other parts of the colonies had been established as "Native Reserves" – i.e. areas where black South African people lived and held land. The white governments decided on a policy which was designed to force young African men away from these areas and into the mines where the labour was needed. All over South Africa poll and hut taxes were introduced – e.g. £2 per head in the Transvaal, £1 per head in Natal. In order to pay the tax, which had to be paid in cash, blacks were forced to seek paid employment and driven out of the non-money economies of their communities. That meant going to the mines.

Off to the compound:

The African workers were contracted for periods of six to twelve months, during which they were paid a wage, and housed in compounds. Contracting workers for a limited length of time ensured that there was a constant supply of unskilled workers, who had no chance of obtaining skills and no chance of developing organizations to resist the conditions imposed. Not only could they not acquire skills in the new industries, but their constant absences from the land meant that they lost the agricultural skills of their families, and their families lost an important source of labour. This new phenomenon of migrant labour steadily altered the whole nature of South African life.

Digging for diamonds, 1872.

What can you tell about the relationship between black and white workers from the diamond rush picture?

Imagine that you have had to go to work in the mines to pay the tax for your family. Write a poem about your new life, or the things you have lost. Would it be an angry or a sad poem?

A compound for African workers at the gold mines. Compounds were surrounded by fences and the workers were virtually imprisoned in them.

THE BOER WAR, 1899-1902

In 1899 war broke out between the British imperial government, supported by the Crown colonies of the Cape and Natal, and the Boer or Afrikaner republics of Transvaal and the Orange Free State. The causes of the war were the struggle for control of the gold reserves in Transvaal, and the determination of the British not to allow any strong (because extremely wealthy) Afrikaner republic to stand in the way of British control of Africa.

The public explanation was that the war was about the demand that the English-speaking "Uitlanders" living in the gold-rush town of Johannesburg should be given equal political rights with the Afrikaners. The Afrikaners were determined to maintain the cultural purity of their state, and wanted no English influences which might result from granting the right to vote to the English-speaking workers in the gold-towns. The British hoped that their enfranchisement would anglicize the republic to the point of enabling some form of control to pass to the imperial government or Cape colony.

Why do you think the Afrikaners were suspicious of the immigrant English? Refer back to the Grahamstown Manifesto (page 13).

A white man's war:

The Barolong and other native tribes near Mafeking [in Cape Colony] were keenly interested in the negotiations that preceded the Boer War. The chiefs continually received information regarding the mobilization of the Boer forces across the [Transvaal] border. This was conveyed to the Magistrate of Mafeking with requests for arms for the purposes of defence. The Magistrate replied each time with confident assurance that the Boers would never cross the boundary into British territory. The Transvaal boundary is only ten or twelve miles from the magistracy. The assurances of the Magistrate made the natives rather restive; the result was that a deputation of Barolong Chiefs had a dramatic interview with the Magistrate, at which the writer acted as interpreter. The chiefs told the Magistrate that they feared he knew very little about war if he thought that belligerents would respect one another's boundaries. He replied in true South African style, that it was a white man's war, and that if the enemy came, His Majesty's white troops would do all the fighting and protect the territories of the chiefs. We remember how Chief Montshiwa and his councillor Joshua Molema went round the Magistrate's chair and crouching behind him said: 'Let us say, for the sake of argument, that your assurances are genuine, and that when trouble begins we hide behind your back like this, and, rifle in hand, you do all the fighting, because you are white; let us say further, that some Dutchmen appear on the scene and they outnumber and shoot you: what would be our course of action then? Are we to run home, put on skirts and hoist the white flag?'

Chief Motshegare pulled off his coat, undid his shirt front and baring his shoulder and showing an old bullet scar, received in the Boer-Barolong war, prior to the British occupation of Bechuanaland, he said: 'Until you can satisfy me that His Majesty's white troops are impervious to bullets, I am going to defend my own wife and children. I have got my rifle at home and all I want is ammunition.'

(*Source:* Plaatje, *Native Life in South Africa*, 1916)

Why do you think the British (and the Boers) were so reluctant to ally with the African communities?

The Boers did cross the frontier on 11 October 1899 and the siege of Mafeking, in which the Barolong played a major part in keeping the garrison supplied with food from cattle-raiding, was to last for 217 days.

Millions of cattle and sheep were slaughtered by the British during the war.

THE CONCENTRATION CAMPS

Elsewhere in South Africa the British gained the upper hand in the war fairly speedily, but victory was to be long delayed. Unable to match the British in money and arms, the Boers had begun to engage in an effective guerilla war. It eventually became clear that the only way the British were going to win the war was by preventing the Boer commando groups from receiving shelter and supplies from Boer farmers. The farmers and their families would have to be cleared from the countryside, and crops and stores burnt. As a result of this policy, thousands of Boer families were rounded up and put in camps.

The Klopper family:

The Klopper family had been captured by some British soldiers and sent on a cattle truck to Kroonstad, along the Vaal river. The family consisted of their mother and eight children:

When we got there we were taken to a sandy hill, a God-forsaken place alongside the Vals river. It was winter then and the river was very low. They gave us a bell tent and said: 'there you are'. Eventually we got a second bell tent and that is where we had to live. There was no protection. In the summer you almost could not live for the flies. And the sanitation was an open hole with small lavatories erected for all the people. You could imagine how disease could spread.

(*Source:* Henning Klopper, quoted in *The White Tribe of Africa*, D. Harrison, BBC Publications, 1981)

Between 1900 and 1902, when the war ended, there were 26,000 deaths in the camps for white people. 20,000 of those who died were children under 16. News of the conditions reached England through the reports of a number of people, one of whom was Emily Hobhouse.

I began to compare a parish I had known at home of 2,000 people where a funeral was an event – and usually of an old person. Here some twenty to twenty-five were carried away daily. . . . The full realisation dawned on me – it was a death rate such as had never been known except in the times of the Great Plague. . .

(*Source:* Emily Hobhouse, *The Brunt of War and Where it Fell*, 1902)

As a result, some improvements were made, such as better water supplies and more medical care.

The death rate in the black concentration camps was just as high. No report was made on them and no protests were registered in Britain.

In what ways do you think this experience of the war might have affected Afrikaner views of British rule?

THE END OF THE WAR

The war ended in the Peace of Vereeniging, signed on 31 May 1902. The Afrikaner republics became Crown colonies administered from Cape Town, but were allowed to restrict the franchise to whites only.

THE BEGINNINGS OF APARTHEID AND THE END OF AFRICAN INDEPENDENCE

"Proper relations between master and servant":

The Transvaal republic established by the trekkers had enshrined in its laws and constitution the same attitudes to black Africans that had caused the Afrikaners to leave the Cape Colony with its more liberal policy on legal and voting rights. Pass laws and residence restrictions were set up and the constitution itself expressly declared that there should be no equality between black and white in Church and State. Black Africans were not allowed to walk on the pavements of the main streets in Pretoria and, when a white African drove by on a country road, the black African stood hat in hand and bowed.

Even in the Cape, where white people were thought to have very liberal attitudes towards black South Africans, that liberalism was itself very limited.

Ought we to put resolutely before us the ideal of equality and try to act up to it, or should we . . . frankly recognise that between us and our coloured countrymen (the very word sounds odd to a South African ear) a great gulf is fixed, and never try to overpass it? . . . The one clue to the maze, we think, is to substitute as far as possible the conception of difference in kind for that of difference in degree. Say not that we are superior and they inferior . . . but simply that we are DIFFERENT, and that the difference involves, as a matter of practical comfort and convenience for both colours, a certain amount of keeping to ourselves. Of course, we shall go on thinking ourselves the superior race; but it is quite open to our coloured friends to do the same. . .

(*Source:* Edmund Garrett, *Cape Times*, 1895)

What is the flaw in the logic of this argument?

Do you think the Afrikaners regarded the British or the Africans as the biggest threat to their existence as a nation in 1902? Why?

THE DEFEAT OF THE ZULU STATE

The mineral revolution had changed Britain's attitude to the existing African states as well. Britain's aim in South Africa by 1875 was to create a federacy of all the colonies, including the Afrikaner republics, under British imperial control. Local British officials were convinced that, in order to achieve this, the Zulu state, the most powerful and wealthy of all the African states, would have to be defeated. It was unlikely that the Cape, the most important and "British" of the colonies, would consent to a federation while the Transvaal and Natal were vulnerable to Zulu attack. The white residents of the Cape would not want to incur the cost of war.

The Zulu king, Cetshwayo, had no intention of launching war against the white colonies, but he suffered both within Zululand and outside from the reputation of the Zulu as warlike and militaristic. In an attempt to pacify his own young troops, the king undertook attacks against black societies on his northern border. But given the determination of the British authorities in Cape Town to engage him in war, war would inevitably come.

In July 1878 some young Zulus chased two Zulu women, accused of adultery, into Natal, captured them and took them back to be executed. The British authorities demanded the return of the boys to face trial and sent an ultimatum to Cetshwayo, of which the terms were designed to be so harsh that it would be bound to be rejected. The Zulu people could hardly believe it:

> You mean to say you are going to destroy Zululand for the sake of two foolish children? The king begs you to show him a favour by allowing him to pay for the crime of the boys. The king begs you to desist from laying Zululand waste for the sake of two foolish children.

(*Source:* Letter from Cetshwayo to the Governor of the Cape, December 1878)

This drawing of a Zulu prisoner appeared in The Graphic *on 2 August 1879. The man on the right (holding the Zulu's shield) was fighting with the British army. The British army had little difficulty in recruiting non-Zulu black soldiers from Natal and the Cape to fight in this war.*

The British army invaded Zululand and at Isandhlwana, on 22 January 1879, suffered one of the most serious defeats ever experienced by an army with guns against an army with hardly any. This sealed the fate of the Zulus. They could win a battle, but not a war, and the British now had to wipe out the humiliation of the defeat. At the battle of Ulundi in July 1879 the Zulus suffered a massive defeat. In August the king was captured. The Zulu kingdom was divided up and left to disintegrate. Finally, in 1887, Zululand was annexed to the British Crown. In 1891 Ceteshwayo wrote:

All what is mine in Zululand has been overturned and spoiled.

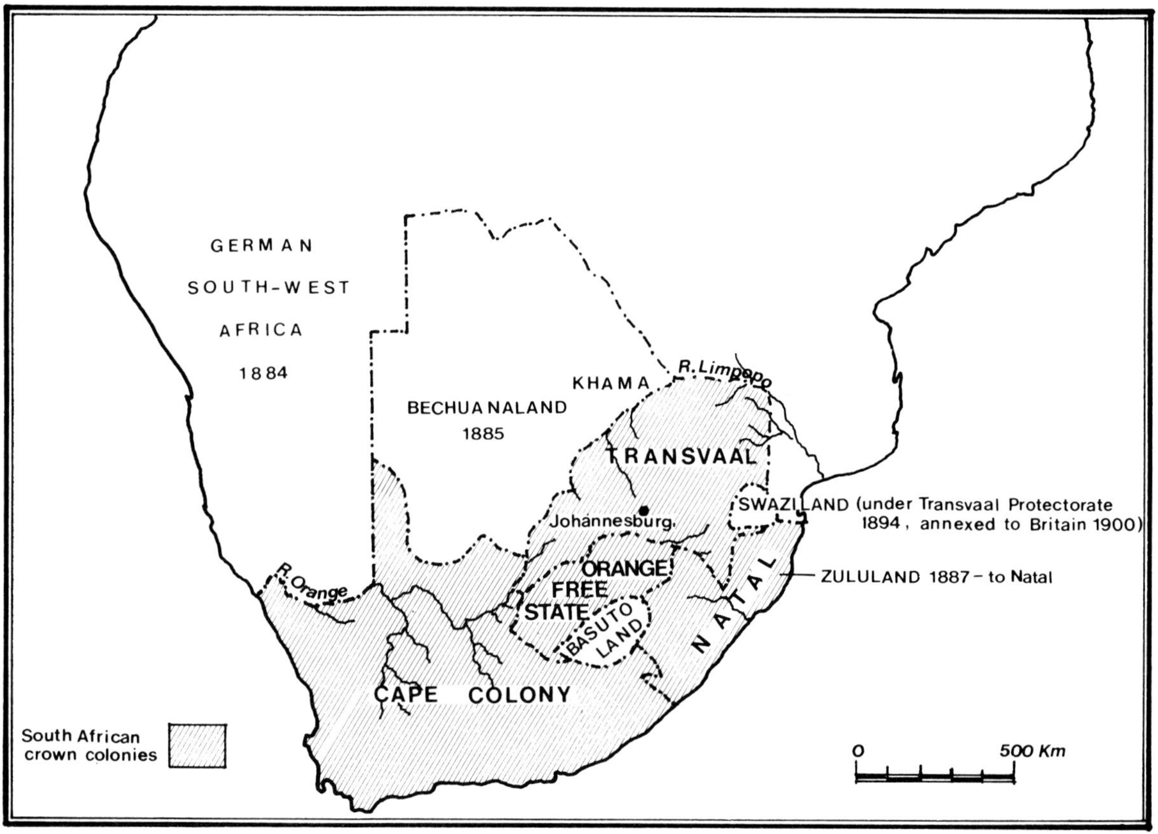

The extent of British control in South Africa, 1902.

ON REFLECTION:

By 1910 Britain had defeated the Boers and the Africans and was effectively in control of almost the whole of Southern Africa. Make a list of all the reasons that enabled Britain to win this position.

Union to Nationalism: 1910-48

UNION OF THE COLONIES

Eight years after the end of the Boer War, the four Crown colonies of South Africa were brought together in the Union of South Africa. The dominant theme of the white history of South Africa during the years following the Union is the assertion of Afrikaner control over the whole of the united dominion of South Africa. This meant, first and foremost, control over the political structures of South Africa, the government and parliament; secondly, control over the land; and finally, control over labour.

AFRIKANER NATIONALISM

Defeated by the British in a costly war, embittered and resentful of the English communities in South Africa, the Afrikaner people of the old Boer republics of the Orange Free State and Transvaal developed a sense of nationhood, national consciousness and cultural unity, which became known as Afrikaner nationalism. This nationalism, rooted in the Great Trek and in the triumph of the founders of the Boer republics against natives and English alike, was to be the most formative influence on the development of the State of South Africa. The persistent image was of the trekkers' Laager: the circle of ox-wagons from inside of which, united in faith, culture and purpose, the Afrikaner fathers, mothers and children had beaten off all opposition. The true Afrikaner knew that, given the strength and commitment of their founding fathers, Afrikanerdom would triumph again.

To achieve political control, Afrikaner nationalists based in the old Boer republics had to wrest power and initiative from the Anglo-Saxon groups who were centred in the Cape and, to a lesser extent, in Natal. To achieve control over the land, the Afrikaners needed to forge an alliance with white employers; for although they were dependent on African migrant labour, the employers could be trusted to prevent African land ownership. And to achieve control over labour, they needed to ally themselves with white workers who were determined to sustain an aristocracy of labour from which non-whites would be excluded. The history of the Afrikaners in this period is one of action and control.

THE STRUGGLE FOR PARLIAMENTARY CONTROL: THE UNION'S CONSTITUTION

The constitution of the Union was based on the British model of government. It was drawn up by a committee on which all the white interests in South Africa were represented. The committee included famous Afrikaners who had led their troops in the war against England just eight years before.

In order to reach agreement on the constitution, several "entrenched" clauses were included; these were clauses which could not be changed without a two-thirds majority of the Parliament being in favour. The clauses were designed to reconcile the competing claims of the colonies and the republics, and to make the Union certain. The colonies and republics were now to become provinces of the new Union.

Why do you think the British and the English South Africans were so eager to ensure the inclusion of the Afrikaner republics in the Union?

THE SOUTH AFRICA ACT, 1909

The Franchise Clause:

35 (1): Parliament may by law prescribe the qualifications which shall be necessary to entitle persons to vote at the election of members of the House of Assembly [The Lower House] but no such law shall disqualify any person in the province of the Cape of Good Hope who, under the laws existing in the Colony of the Cape of Good Hope at the establishment of the Union, is or may become capable of being registered as a voter from being so registered in the province of the Cape of Good Hope by reason of his race or colour only, unless the Bill be passed by both Houses of Parliament sitting together, and at the third reading be agreed by not less than two thirds of the total number of members of both houses. . .

The Clause allowing Rural Bias:

40 (3): The Commission [making the constituency boundaries] shall give due consideration to:

(a) community or diversity of interests;
(b) means of communication
(c) physical features
(d) existing electoral boundaries
(e) sparsity and density of population

in such manner that, while taking the quota of voters as the basis of division, the Commission may, whenever they deem it necessary, depart therefrom, but in no case to any greater extent than fifteen per centum more or fifteen per centum less than the quota.

The Language Clause:

137 Both the English and Dutch languages shall be official languages of the Union, and shall be treated on a footing of equality, and possess and enjoy equal freedom, rights and privileges. . .

The Entrenching Clause:

152 Amendment of Act:
. . . And provided further that no repeal or alteration of the provisions contained in this section . . . or in sections 35, and 137 shall be valid unless the Bill embodying such repeal . . . shall be passed by both Houses of Parliament sitting together and at the third reading be agreed by not less than two thirds of the total numbers of members of both houses.

Why do you think the Cape representatives insisted on entrenching their system of voting qualifications?

Why do you think the Afrikaners wanted to ensure the equal status of Dutch?

What might be the effect of allowing the commissioners to make rural constituencies with up to thirty per cent fewer voters than urban ones?

THE SHIFTING SANDS OF POWER

South African Assembly: Election results, 1910-48:

DATE	GOVERNMENT	PRIME MINISTER	NUMBER OF SEATS	COALITION PARTY (SEATS)	MAIN OPPOSITION PARTY (SEATS)
1910	S.A.P.	Botha	68	none	Unionist
1915	S.A.P.	Botha	54	Unionist	Nationalist (27)
1920	S.A.P.	Smuts	41	Unionist	Nats. (44)
1921	S.A.P.	Smuts	79	none	Nats. (45)
1924	Nats.	Herzog	63	Labour (18)	S.A.P. (53)
1929	Nats.	Herzog	78	Labour (5)	S.A.P. (61)
1933	Nats.	Herzog	75	none	S.A.P. (61)
1938	United	Herzog	111	none	Pur. Nats. (27)
1943	United	Smuts	89	none	Nats. (43)
1948	Nats.	Malan	70	Afrikaner (9)	U.P. (65)

NOTES

S.A.P.: South African Party: coalition of Afrikaner provincial parties with some support from English colonies.

Nationalists 1915-33: an Afrikaner party split from the S.A.P. in 1912, because S.A.P.'s policies not sufficiently pro-Afrikaner.

Nationalists 1934 on (initially Purified Nationalists): Afrikaner party formed when Nationalist leader Herzog united his party with the S.A.P. to form the United Party.

United Party: formed 1934 by union of Smuts' S.A.P. and Herzog's wing of the Nationalists. Formed partly because of economic crisis and the need to create a firm government. A two-thirds majority was now available in Parliament for amending the constitution and in 1934 the Native Representation Act was passed which removed African voters from the electoral roll and prevented new voters being added to the existing roll.

Unionist: 1910-21: party of English-speaking white colonists from Cape and Natal. Merged with S.A.P.

Labour: white working-class party advocating industrial colour-bar. Lost influence after 1924 when industrial colour-bar introduced (see page 30).

Afrikaner: split from United Party in 1939 over participation in WW2: led by Herzog.

If you study the table of election results and the notes carefully, you will see that splits in the ruling party were primarily caused by Afrikaners feeling that the party was insufficiently committed to the rights of Afrikaners, as opposed to the English-speaking areas. After a while, this more extreme Afrikaner group gains enough support from the white electorate to move into government.

Look back at Clause 40 of the South Africa Act (page 26). Why might it help this process?

DIE KAFFIR OP SY PLEK ("Keep the black man in his place")

At the time of the Union, in the Boer republics, there already existed extensive legislation designed to preserve the dominance of the white people over the black South Africans. In the British colonies, too, there were laws designed to force blacks onto the labour market. The creation of the Union, and the new government's need to maintain support among the white Afrikaners, now gave the opportunity for such legislation to be extended throughout South Africa.

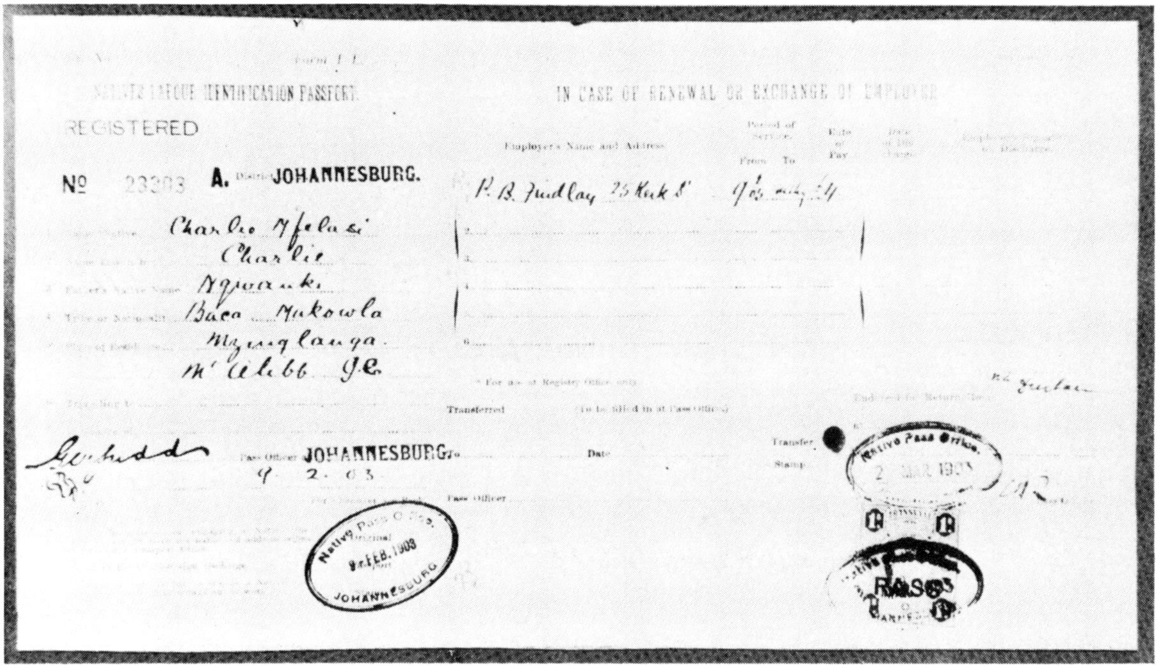

A pass for a black worker in Johannesburg, Transvaal, 1903.

It would be impossible, in the space of this book, to look in detail at all the controlling laws. We shall concentrate on just two, which represent the legislation – the Native Land Act and the Mines and Works Amendment Act.

THE NATIVE LAND ACT, 1913

The Boer War had considerably worsened the problems of the landless white Afrikaners. The destruction of farms by the British army and the financial difficulties faced as a result by land-owning Afrikaners had forced the "bijwoners" (tenants-at-will living on the land of wealthier kinsmen) into the towns or into starvation. Their neighbours could no longer support them.

Now that Africa had been divided up and frontiers drawn, it was impossible for the Afrikaners to solve their land shortage problem by trekking out, as they had done in the past. Another difficulty for the Afrikaners was that the efficiency of African peasant farmers was enabling the latter to purchase and live off land; they refused to work as labourers on the land of the plantation-owning whites. They had no need to, as their own land produced enough to support them. In addition, there was a racial or cultural anxiety among whites about the possible results of poor white Afrikaners being forced to live in the mixed slums of the new cities.

Afrikaner poverty:

I have observed instances in which the children of Afrikaner families were running around as naked as Kaffirs in Congoland. We have knowledge today of Afrikaner girls, so poor they work for coolies and Chinese. We know of white men and women who live married and unmarried with Coloureds. They are all our flesh and blood; they carry our names; they are Afrikaners all of them; they are the sons and daughters of Huguenots and the children of martyrs.

(*Source:* from a speech made in 1916 by D.F. Malan, Editor of *Die Burger*)

The Native Land Act defined and guaranteed areas which were to be set aside for black Africans, in which they could purchase and lease land. They were not permitted to own land outside these areas. (The Cape was exempt from this legislation as to attack black land-ownership there would interfere with the voting rights and need a two-thirds majority.) The area allocated to the blacks consisted of some 7% of South Africa's total area. Non-white South Africans made up 67.3% of the population. White farmers who failed to evict their black squatters or tenants from the land faced a fine of £100.

The dispossessed:

In 1914 a Petition for Land was addressed to the Native Land Commissioner. It was one of many.

. . . There is no place where we can make a permanent home; we do not like our children to be homeless wanderers all the days of our life. . . . The position is the same for Kaffir, Fingo, Hottentot, Basuto and Zulu. We are equally under one yoke. . . . We earnestly entreat the Government to set apart for us land where we can establish homes. We appeal to the Government which is over black and white alike and should shelter and protect all its subjects as a hen gathers under her wings her little ones without regard to their colour.
Signed: M.K. Mancobo (Pastor)
J. Ntongwana (Secretary)

Using all you have learned of the attitudes and needs of the white communities, explain why the Land Act was passed and why this sort of appeal went unheeded.

Postscript:

In 1936 the Native Trust and Land Act designated a further amount of land for Africans, and arranged for a trust to buy up this land with money set aside from time to time by Parliament. Technically, this increased to 13.7% the area available for Africans to own and farm. This land had still not all been acquired for African use in 1986. Africans now constitute about 70% of the population.

THE MINES AND WORKS AMENDMENT ACT, 1926

In 1924 the S.A.P. government of Smuts was defeated in the election by a coalition of Herzog's Nationalist Party and the white, English-speaking Labour Party. One of the many reasons for this lay in a particularly bitter strike that had occurred in the gold mines in 1922. In an attempt to cut their labour costs, the mine-owners had proposed opening skilled grades of jobs to African mine-workers, thus reducing wages. To the Afrikaners, who had increasingly been employed in the mines as they had been driven from the land, and who were forming a new Afrikaner working class, this proposed move represented an extension of the problem they had been encountering for one hundred and fifty years: the "English" using the blacks to get the better of the Afrikaners.

The Labour Party, concerned to protect the interests of white workers, and the Nationalist Party, concerned to protect the position of poor, landless Afrikaners, united on a platform of entrenching and extending the laws that reserved skilled occupations on the basis of the colour of the workers' skin.

Look back at Retief's Manifesto (page 13). Is there evidence there that Retief accepted the idea that the English liked "getting the better of the Afrikaners"?

The Europeans must keep to a standard of living which shall meet the demands of white civilisation. Civilisation and standards of living always go hand in hand. Thus a white cannot exist on a native wage scale, because that means that he has to give up his own standard of living and take on the standard of living of the native. In short the white man becomes a white kaffir.

(*Source:* Herzog, Leader of the National Party, quoted in *The White Tribe of Africa*, D. Harrison, BBC Publications, 1981)

THE WHITE WORKERS

In 1927 a British Labour peer described the position of the Labour Party in the following way:

European aristocracy:

The white wages, it is uncompromisingly recognised and stated, can only be paid on condition of Natives alone being employed for all unskilled and semi-skilled labour, and being paid at a sweated wage. . . . This direct dependence of the white worker's very high wages (the highest in the world) upon the very low wages of the Native labourer, is the secret of the philosophy of the industrial colour bar . . . recently embodied in legislation at the demand of the white South African Labour Party. . . . The Labour Party may not, perhaps, desire to exploit the Native, but it is doing so, through the operation of the conditions thus begotten. Not unnaturally, it prefers doing so to having its own wages reduced, which in the evolved conditions under which alone the mining industry can be fully maintained, is practically the only alternative.

(*Source:* Lord Oliver, *The Anatomy of African Misery*, 1927)

Did the Afrikaners and the Labour Party members have a different attitude to black workers? Did this make any difference to their policies towards black workers?

THE "CIVILIZED" LABOUR POLICY

The Act which the Herzog government passed in 1926 empowered the Ministry of Labour to implement a colour-bar in employment. The law now ensured that white workers only would hold the best-paid, most powerful and most skilled jobs. As a result, the Labour Party ceased to have a significant policy to offer and declined in political influence. The Nationalists had secured an increased number of jobs, in railways, the civil service and other industries, as well as in mines, for the growing numbers of landless Afrikaners. The black Africans' rights and interests had been further undermined.

Do you think the policies of the Nationalists and the Labour Party were particularly directed against black Africans? In other words, were they explicitly racist – or were they directed against other "enemies"?

BLACK AFRICANS AND THE UNION

The black people of South Africa were denied any access to the institutions of political control under the constitution of the Union. Their history from 1910 to 1948 is dominated by their efforts to modify and influence policies instituted by the whites. This period also sees their first attempts to develop organizations and policies exploring the political and economic influence they could assert outside the formally constituted political system. Black African history in these years is a history of reaction.

The Union of South Africa and the creation of the new state on a firm basis of white supremacy led many black South Africans to realize that a national African organization was now necessary to challenge and hopefully change the laws governing their lives: the pass laws; the limited franchise; the poll taxes and stringent anti-black laws in the ex-Afrikaner republics.

In January 1912, groups of black Africans from all over the Union, dominated by chiefs, priests, journalists and lawyers (i.e. the more powerful and better-educated black Africans), met in Johannesburg and founded the South African Native Congress (S.A.N.C.). The moving spirit behind the organization was Poxley Ka Izaka Seme, a barrister trained in New York and London.

Seme's call for unity:

The demon of racialism, the aberrations of the Xhosa-Fingo feud, the animosity that exists between the Zulus and Tongas, between the Basutos and every other Native must be buried and forgotten. . . . We are one people. These divisions, these jealousies, are the cause of all our woes and of all our backwardness and ignorance today.

(*Source:* Seme, *Imvo, 24 October 1911)*

Addressing the people gathered at the meeting in Johannesburg, Seme outlined his purpose in the following way:

Chiefs of Royal blood and gentlemen of our race, we have gathered here to consider and discuss a scheme which my colleagues and I have decided to place before you. We have discovered that in the land of their birth, Africans are treated as hewers of wood and drawers of water. The white people of this country have formed what is known as the Union of South Africa – a union in which we have no voice in the making of laws and no part in the administration. We have called you, therefore, to this conference so that we can together find ways and means of forming OUR national union for the purpose of creating national unity and defending our rights and privileges.

(*Source:* quoted in Mary Benson, *South Africa. The Struggle for a Birth Right*, Penguin, 1966)

The S.A.N.C. resolved to pursue its policies to defend black rights by resolution, peaceful protest, propaganda, deputations, education and united action.

The A.N.C. delegation in London to protest at the Land Act, 1914.

In what ways do you think the kinds of people the conference members were might have affected the way the S.A.N.C. was to work?

THE I.C.U. The Industrial and Commercial Workers Union of South Africa (I.C.U.), founded in Cape Town in 1919, by Clements Kadalie, became the most powerful mass black African movement of the inter-war years. It is hard to assess its membership accurately, but it may well have been as high as 100,000 at its peak in 1926, and many thousands more were sympathizers and supporters.

The top of a page of I.C.U. notepaper.

Despite its huge membership, the I.C.U. did not achieve many concrete benefits for Africans, either in terms of improving their conditions of work or in securing political rights. By 1930, when Kadalie led his last strike among the dock-workers of East London, the I.C.U. was weak, divided and in disarray. The reasons for this are complex and legion. Internal divisions among the leadership, a lack of clear policy as to whether to be a political party or a trade union, government repression, lack of support from white workers (who were often in the forefront when breaking I.C.U. strikes), inefficient administration: all played their part. But this should not lead us to underestimate the importance of the I.C.U. as an example to future generations. It showed Africans that they could unite, organize and take positive steps, even if they could not yet win concessions.

Why do you think the I.C.U. was potentially a more powerful organization than the S.A.N.C. in the inter-war years?

GOVERNMENT RESPONSE TO BLACK PROTEST

Official figures of deaths after police fired on black crowds:

1920:	Rand: African mineworkers' strike	8 killed
1920:	Port Elizabeth: Protest over I.C.U. arrests	21 killed
1921:	Queenstown: Religious group refusing to vacate land	163 killed
1922:	Namibia: Refusal to pay dog tax	100 killed
1925:	Bloemfontein: Punitive action in location	5 killed
1929:	Durban: Trade union office attacked	5 killed
1930:	Durban: Pass-burning campaign	4 killed

How reliable do you think these figures are?

In his book Time Longer than Rope, *Edward Roux describes the deaths at Bloemfontein as "another of those periodic massacres of Natives by which civilised white South Africa asserts its rights to rule over the inferior races". How reliable a judgement do you think that is?*

THE SECOND WORLD WAR

South Africa's decision to enter the war in alliance with Britain in 1939 split the United Party. Smuts, who supported the war, won the debate in Parliament by two votes. Herzog, with widespread Afrikaner support, argued for neutrality, was defeated, and left the government. Many more extreme Afrikaners hoped (and some worked) for a German victory.

Black South Africans were recruited into the armed forces, but as non-combatants: they were forbidden to carry arms or take part in the fighting. Many blacks were needed also to replace the skilled white South Africans who had joined up, and so the colour-bar at work was relaxed. Many more blacks were encouraged to move to the towns to work in the war industries and the developing manufacturing industries.

By the end of the war, black attitudes and aspirations had been subtly altered. The Second World War was presented by the Allies as a moral crusade: a struggle for freedom and human rights for all people. This message was not lost on the South African black community. On a social and economic level, moving to the towns and being encouraged to undertake skilled jobs had reinforced a sense of unity among black people and developed their self-confidence. In contrast to this the English South Africans remained complacent, convinced that the changes in the world had no relevance to South Africa, and the Afrikaners were once more determined to wrest political power from the English-speaking whites. The outcome was the Nationalist victory of 1948, and the black opposition to it, which have dominated South African history ever since.

ON REFLECTION:

Why do you think Seme placed so much emphasis on unity among black South Africans in his call to found the S.A.N.C.?

The Establishment of Apartheid: 1948-60

The election of the Nationalist government in 1948 ushered in a new phase in South African history. The government of the new Prime Minister, D.F. Malan, was made up, for the first time, of all Afrikaner ministers. The policy on which they had been elected to government was that of *Apartheid*, or separate development of all races, white, coloured, Indian and African. The following decade saw the systematic implementation of this policy through wide-ranging legislation. People of non-white classification were forcibly removed across hundreds of miles to native reserves, while park benches were divided into those which whites could sit on and those which non-whites could sit on. Faced with such a coherent and persistent onslaught on their position in South African society, non-whites were galvanized into organized and determined opposition and achieved a level of unity and purpose not experienced before, even in the days of the I.C.U. In this chapter we shall look first at the basis of Apartheid and at its implementation, and then at the development of black opposition. The issues looked at are necessarily selective. They are designed to provoke further thought and research and cannot hope to cover all the issues that were central to people's lives at this time.

THE ROOTS OF APARTHEID

We have seen how, from their earliest beginnings, the Boer republics of South Africa followed policies designed to ensure that black South Africans took second place in their societies. We have seen how both English and socialist whites followed policies which kept black labour in the poorest jobs in the industries of South Africa; and also how, in questions of land-ownership and farming, the position of the white (usually Boer) farmer was protected at the expense of the African farmers. Legislation was passed when necessary to confirm the position of the white communities in law. South Africa at this stage was a society that practised segregation of races and discriminated in both law and attitude against non-white (particularly African) citizens. But Apartheid is different from segregation and discrimination: different in degree and in fundamentals.

Afrikaner nationalism, which traced its roots back to the Great Trek, faced something of a crisis in the 1930s. Despite the fact that every Prime Minister since Union had been an Afrikaner, and despite legislation to protect Afrikaner (and other white) interests in land, labour and political rights, the position of the Afrikaner people vis-à-vis the Anglo-Saxon whites was deteriorating. The economic crisis of the 1930s had made rural poverty much worse, forcing thousands of poor white families off the land and into the cities.

In the cities, two things impressed themselves on the Afrikaners and made them feel that no advance had been made since 1900. They were foreigners here: despite the equality of English and Afrikanse (the Dutch dialect spoken by the Afrikaners) enshrined in the constitution (see page 26) the cities were predominantly Anglo-Saxon. The signs were in English, and English was spoken in the shops. The best jobs were held by the English, justice was administered in English. The best housing areas were English, the best schools, the theatres. The religion was Anglican. The Afrikaners did not belong.

The newly arrived families were competing with the black communities for jobs and living space. Worse, the Indian and coloured communities were more prosperous and more privileged. Even Prime Minister Herzog, the man responsible for removing Africans from the voting roll in 1936, argued that coloured people were equal to whites. The laws preventing marriage and sexual relationships between people of different races did not apply to coloureds. The white working class of Afrikaners were coming face to face with the black workers, and were encountering a society in which they had no power, wealth or prestige, and in which non-whites were above them on the economic and social ladder.

The response of the Afrikaner leaders was to develop a set of ideas that was designed to protect and empower the Afrikaner peoples once and for all. This new ideology contained three strands: the idea of the Afrikaner nation; the sanctification of this nation by God; and the preservation of the nation through racial purity.

The Afrikaner nation:

To Afrikanerdom belong only those who by virtue of blood, soil, culture, tradition, belief, calling form an organic unitary society. . .

In the future Afrikaner national state the undivided power granted by God rests with the Afrikaner state authority . . . power shall only be exercised in accordance with the principles of law contained in the Word of God, and the natural legal ordinations as consistently revealed in history.

(*Source:* Dr P.J. Meyer, theoretician of Afrikaner nationalism, 1942, quoted in *The Puritans in Africa*, W. de Klerk, London, 1975)

The Word of God:

Members of the Dutch Reformed Church, to which most Afrikaners belonged, preached sermons on Apartheid as a reflection of God's law, using such Biblical texts as these:

When the Most High gave the nations their inheritance
when he divided the sons of man
he fixed their bounds according to the numbers of the sons of God.

(*Source: The Bible*, Deuteronomy 32:8)

From one single stock he not only created the whole human race so that they could occupy the entire earth, but he decreed how long each nation should flourish and what the boundaries of its territories should be.

(*Source: The Bible,* Acts 17:26)

Racial purity:

The more consistently the policy of Apartheid could be applied, the greater would be the security for the purity of our blood and the surer unadulterated European racial survival . . . total racial separation . . . is the most consistent application of the Afrikaner idea of racial apartheid.

(*Source:* Dr G. Cronje, theoretician of Apartheid, 1945, quoted in *The Puritans in Africa*, London, 1975)

Have Afrikaner ideas changed much since the Great Trek (see page 13)?

Resolution of the Congress of the People (Volkskongres), Bloemfontein, September 1944:

That it is in the interests of the white and non-white populations of South Africa that a policy of apartheid be followed, so that each of the non-white population groups will find the opportunity to develop according to its own characteristics, in its own area, so as to acquire, eventually, full control over their own affairs. . . . That it is the Christian duty of the whites to act as guardians over the non-white races until such time as they have reached the level where they can look after their own affairs.

Look up the story of the Tower of Babel in the Bible (Genesis 11) and explain how it could be used to justify a theory of racial Apartheid.

Why do you think the involvement of religious ideas in Apartheid made it a more powerful idea?

In 1945 Apartheid was adopted as the official policy of Malan's National Party. In 1948 they won the election by a majority of 5, in alliance with Herzog's Afrikaner Party.

APARTHEID IN PRACTICE

The main architect of Apartheid in practice was Dr H. Verwoerd, an Afrikaner intellectual who became Minister for Native Affairs in Malan's government in 1950 and Prime Minister in 1958.

SEGREGATION: THE GROUP AREAS ACT (1950) AND THE RESETTLEMENT OF NATIVES ACT (1954)

The logic of Apartheid (separate development) required that all the racial groups in South Africa should be separated from each other. Dr Verwoerd explained how this policy would work in practice, to the Native Representative Council, at its last meeting before it was abolished in 1950. The Council had been set up before the war, as a vehicle for conveying the views of black South Africans to the government.

The only possible way out [of inevitable conflict between the races] is to adopt a development divorced from each other. . . . Its starting point is the Native territories. . . . What length of time it will take the Bantu in the reserves to advance to . . . self-government will depend on his own industry. . .

In the countryside there has, up to the present, not been a clash of social interests. . . . Apart from the removal of Black spots . . . the policy of apartheid is not so much an issue at this juncture. . .

Finally there are the implications of the apartheid policy in respect of the European cities . . . not only must there be separation between European and non-European residential areas, but also that the different non-European groups . . . shall live in their own residential areas.

(*Source:* Verwoerd: address to N.R.C., 5 December 1950)

Why do you think there was no Apartheid practised between Afrikaner and Anglo-Saxon South Africans?

These maps and diagrams show how the principles of Apartheid are applied to living areas throughout the country as a whole, and in the urban areas.
a. The areas designated as the "homelands" (bantustans) of the African people of South Africa consist of many small and scattered pieces, based on the Native Land Acts 1913 and 1936. Today black Africans make up 70% of the total population. The land allocated to them is about 13.6% of the total.
b. Group areas in Cape Town, introduced by the Government Act, 1950.
c. The division into different language group areas of the Daveytown Township near Benoni, East Rand.

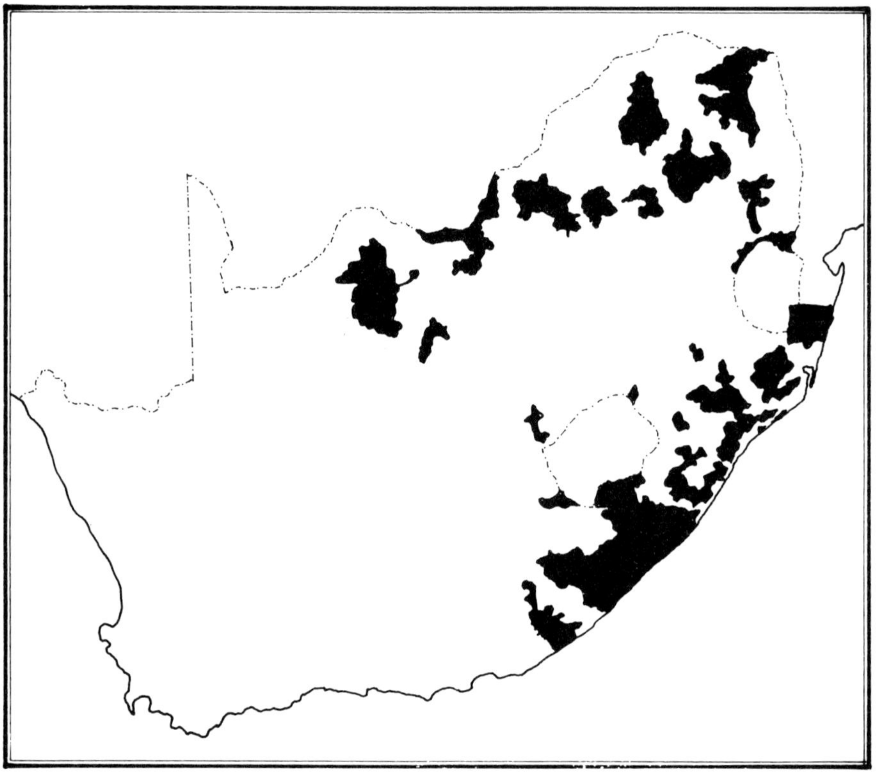

a.

b.

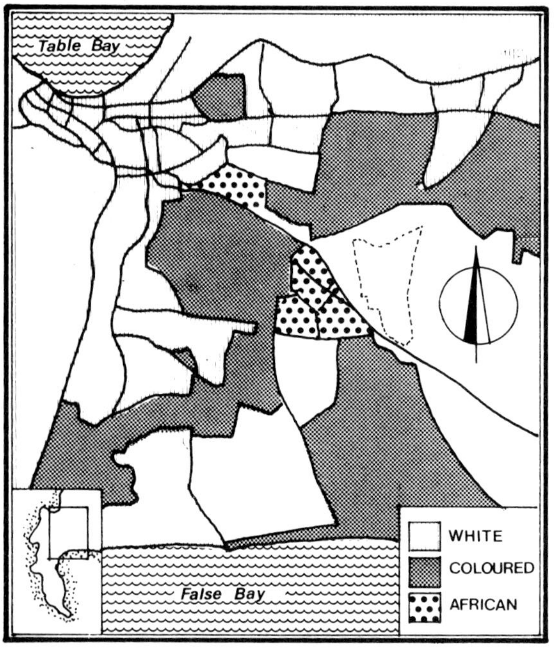

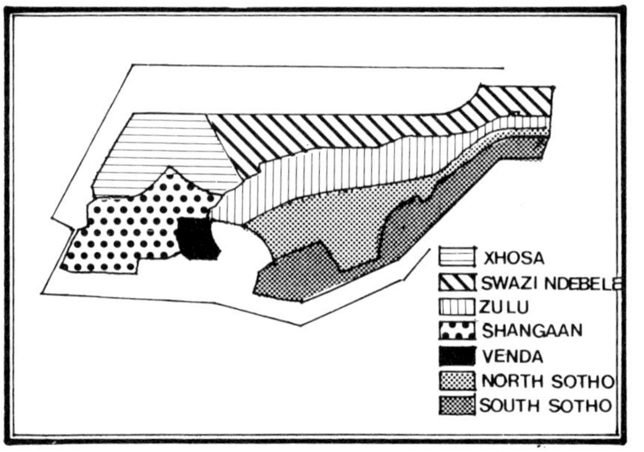

c.

The areas allocated to the Africans by the two acts was the area already allocated to them by the Native Trust and Land Act of 1936. Not all this land has yet been acquired for Africans (1986).

What do you think might have been the point of subdividing the African areas of the towns – often called "townships" – along "ethnic" lines?

Read Naught For Your Comfort *by Trevor Huddleston, which recounts the removal of residents from Sophiatown as a result of the Resettlement of Natives Act.*

EDUCATION: THE BANTU EDUCATION ACT (1953)

Schools:

My [Native Affairs] department's policy is that Education should stand with both feet in the reserves and have its roots in the spirit and being of Bantu society. There Bantu Education must be able to give itself complete expression and there it will be called upon to perform its real service. The Bantu must be guided to serve his own community in all respects. There is no place for him in the European community above the level of certain forms of labour. Within his own community however all doors are open. . . . Until now he has been subjected to a school system which drew him away from his own community and misled him by showing him the green pastures of European society in which he was not allowed to graze. . . . What is the point of teaching a Bantu child Mathematics when he cannot use it in practice?

(*Source:* Dr H.F. Verwoerd, June 1954)

The training and payment of teachers:

The government took over the training of black teachers who would previously have been to training colleges financed by European churches. New pay scales were issued, making salaries considerably lower than previous ones (and much lower than white teachers received).

Good race relations cannot exist when education is given under the control of people who create wrong expectations on the part of the Native himself. . . . The Bantu teacher serves the Bantu community and his salary must be fixed accordingly [and] possibly be less favourable than the existing scales.

(*Source:* Verwoerd, 1953)

Government spending on school education, 1959-60:

RACE	AMOUNT SPENT PER HEAD
White	R125
Coloured and Indian	R70
African	R14

What effect do you think this policy for education would have on the standards of education for the non-white children?

OPPOSITION: THE CONGRESS OF THE PEOPLE AND THE FREEDOM CHARTER

The imposition of Apartheid began to draw together all those people – white, coloured, Indian and African – who were opposed to the system. In 1954 a meeting was held of the African National Congress (renamed from the South African Native Congress), the South African Indian Congress, the South African Coloured People's Organization, the Congress of Democrats, and the non-racial South African Congress of Trade Unions. They planned to hold another meeting the following year, to be called the Congress of the People, at which a Freedom Charter outlining the demands of the people would be discussed. The Charter was to be drawn up through discussions and meetings involving as many people as possible and organized by volunteers.

Listen friend . . .:

Yes it's you I mean – Armit, Amina, Marimoothu, or whatever your name is – What are you interested in? Football? Cricket?. . . Do you like reading? Do you want a chance to learn a proper trade or profession?

Whatever it is, there are thousands like you, young South Africans who never have the chance to get the kind of education they should. . .

Every young person born in this country is entitled to certain things, no matter who he is or what his race. . .

Millions of South Africans during the coming weeks . . . are going to discuss what they want from life. . . . They are going to speak of freedom, and draw up their demands into a Freedom Charter. . .

A call has gone out . . . for a greater assembly of elected representatives of all races . . . who will draw up the demands of all the people into the FREEDOM CHARTER. . .

How can such a mighty Congress be organised? Only through a band of voluntary helpers who will cover the country from end to end. . .

It is a job for you, Ahmed, Ismail, or whatever your name is. Don't sit back and dream of what you would like from life. Write your hopes into the Freedom Charter! . . .

FILL IN THIS FORM – NOW!

(*Source:* from a pamphlet issued by the South African Indian Youth Congress)

The Congress of the People was held in a field outside Johannesburg on 25 and 26 June 1955 and nearly 3,000 delegates attended from all over the country. Even the government had been invited to send a delegation. (When the police turned up on the Sunday afternoon the people joked that the government had sent their delegation.)

THE FREEDOM CHARTER

Preamble:

We, the people of South Africa, declare for all our country and the world to know:

That South Africa belongs to all that live in it, black and white, and that no government can justly claim authority unless it is based on the will of the people;

That our people have been robbed of their birthright to land, liberty and

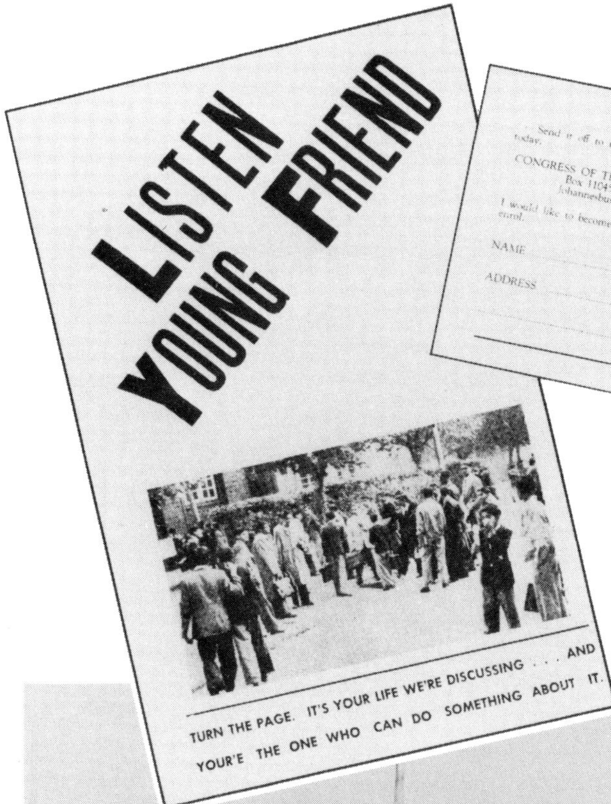

LISTEN YOUNG FRIEND

TURN THE PAGE. IT'S YOUR LIFE WE'RE DISCUSSING . . . AND YOUR'E THE ONE WHO CAN DO SOMETHING ABOUT IT.

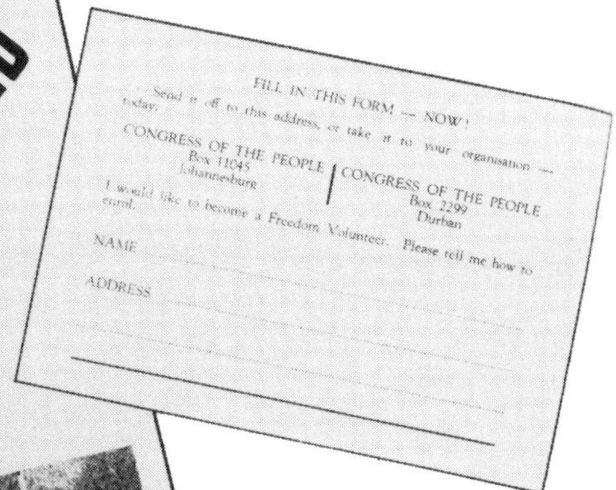

FILL IN THIS FORM — NOW!

Send it off to this address, or take it to your organisation — today.

CONGRESS OF THE PEOPLE
Box 11045
Johannesburg

CONGRESS OF THE PEOPLE
Box 2299
Durban

I would like to become a Freedom Volunteer. Please tell me how to enrol.

NAME

ADDRESS

The pamphlet issued by the South African Indian Youth Congress.

A view of the platform at the Congress of the people.

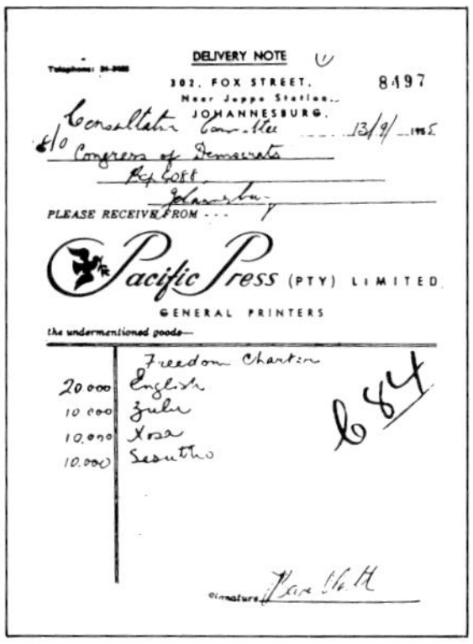

DELIVERY NOTE

302, FOX STREET,
Near Jeppe Station,
JOHANNESBURG.

8497

PLEASE RECEIVE FROM

Pacific Press (PTY) LIMITED
GENERAL PRINTERS

the undermentioned goods

Freedom Charter
20,000 English
10,000 Zulu
10,000 Xosa
10,000 Sesutho

A bill for 50,000 copies of the Freedom Charter, in different languages.

peace by a form of government founded on injustice and inequality;
That our country will never be prosperous or free until all our people live in brotherhood, enjoying equal rights and opportunities;
That only a democratic state, based on the will of the people, can secure to all their birthright without distinction of colour, race, sex or belief;
And therefore, we the people of South Africa, black and white, together equals, countrymen and brothers adopt this FREEDOM CHARTER...

(*Source:* from The Freedom Charter adopted at the Congress of the People, 26 June 1955)

Published 23 December 1956.

IS FREEDOM CHARTER TREASON?

Crown Refuses To Answer Defence Query

To All Our Readers—
PEACE AND FREEDOM IN THE NEW YEAR

NEW AGE

Vol. 3, No. 9 Registered at the G.P.O. as a newspaper.

SOUTHERN EDITION Thursday, December 27, 1956 PRICE 3d.

JOHANNESBURG.

WHAT EXACTLY CONSTITUTES THE CHARGE OF TREASON AGAINST THE 154 ACCUSED WHO APPEARED AT THE PREPARATORY EXAMINATION AT THE DRILL HALL LAST WEEK?

THE CROWN IS NOT YET PREPARED TO ANSWER THIS QUESTION.

In reply to questions by defence counsel at the end of the proceedings last week, Mr. J. C. van Niekerk, for the Crown, said he was not in a position at this stage to say what allegations were going to be made at the end of the preparatory examination.

Mr. V. C. Berrange, for the defence, asked whether the Crown maintained that the Freedom Charter was treasonable or not.

Mr. van Niekerk: That is a question that could be decided after all the evidence has been led.

Mr. Berrange: My only object in raising this matter is that the Freedom Charter has been circulated in tens of thousands all over the country since 1954, and if it was treasonable one would have expected action to be taken before now.

The outline of the Crown case was given by Mr. van Niekerk, who read slowly and haltingly from a document of 53 typed pages. Reporters who asked for copies of the address were told it was badly typed, and he had not read everything in it.

The gist of the Crown case, said Mr. van Niekerk, was that at meetings held all over the Union and in documents the accused advocated, propagated and preached a Marxist-Leninist account of society and the State, a Marxist-Leninist interpretation of history and contemporary politics, and called for the establishment of a people's democratic state based on the principles of the system in the Soviet Union, the people's democracies of Eastern Europe and China.

They preached that imperialism and colonialism should be destroyed and advocated the drawing up of a Freedom Charter as the basis of a people's democracy in South Africa. The Crown would allege that the accused relied on the aid of outside countries to establish this people's democracy.

LIBERATION MOVEMENT

Mr. van Niekerk said that all the organisations named in the indictment constituted a national liberation movement, and it would be alleged that the steps set out in the Freedom Charter were steps in the direction of a Communist state and, if necessary, a prelude to revolution.

The evidence would be that the liberation movement relied on extra-parliamentary action to achieve its object because it did not see any alternative under the existing constitution.

The Communist Party manifesto was quoted in support of the Crown allegation that Communists stood for violent revolution and the destruction of capitalist oppressors. Mr. van Niekerk then quoted from speeches and documents to show:

(a) That some of the accused taught that the South African state

(Continued on page 4)

"AFRIKA!"—A section of the crowd waves farewell to the Black Maria after the first day's "treason" bearing. Notice the raised thumb through the bars of the van.

Brutal Police Attacks At Drill Hall

JOHANNESBURG.

BOTH the second and third days of the "treason" hearings at the Drill Hall were marked by ugly scenes of police violence against the thousands of South Africans of all races who had come to stand by their leaders.

The crowd ringed the hall in queues seven deep and then spilled over the pavements, completely blocking Twist and Quartz Streets, while heavily armed police stood by.

Forewarned by leaders of the People's Defence Committee against provocation (a leaflet distributed outside the Court on the first day urged people to give the police no [illegible]

But that did not deter the police from ruthless action against them.

SHOOTING

Proceedings during the second day of the mass treason trial in the Drill Hall were dramatically interrupted when the sound of shooting was heard outside. Those in the hall immediately realised that police had opened fire on the vast crowd outside, which had throughout the first day resisted all attempts at provocation, and cries of anger and indignation echoed through the Court, so that the Magistrate, Mr. Wessels had to adjourn.

The trouble began when the police under Col. [illegible] trying to push the thousands of people who were unable to gain admission to the hall, away from the entrance [illegible]

After the Congress of the People hundreds of thousands of copies of the charter were distributed in all languages.

Imagine you were one of the delegates at the Congress of the People. Write an entry in your diary describing the occasion and what it meant to you.

The government reacts:

The growing success of the opposition movement resulted in the arrest of 156 leaders of the Congress who were charged with High Treason, the penalty for which was death. Those arrested, on the night of 5 December 1956, included men and women of all races and colours. The basis of the charge was the Freedom Charter, and the argument was that it represented a communist conspiracy to overthrow the state by violent means.

As the trial progressed, it was found that the charges against more and more of the defendants could not be substantiated. In March 1961 the last 30 defendants were found not guilty and released. The trial had lasted over four years.

THE SHARPEVILLE MASSACRE

The pass laws had been in existence in South Africa in one form or another for hundreds of years. Basically, they were a technique for controlling the movement and employment of non-white people. They had long been a focus of non-white resistance. The Indian Congress movement, founded by Gandhi in 1893, had led campaigns against the laws. Attempts to impose passes on women in the years around the First World War had been successfully resisted.

Under Apartheid, the pass laws became a more sophisticated technique for ensuring that non-white people could not work, live or travel in any area not designated for their use. In the early 1950s the A.N.C. had led a defiance campaign against all the laws of Apartheid, of which the passes became a symbol. In the mid-fifties, 20,000 women had marched through the streets of Pretoria to protest at the imposition of passes on them.

Women protest:

Men are born into the system, and it is as if it has become a life tradition that they carry passes. We as women have seen the treatment our men have – when they leave home in the mornings you are not sure they will come back. We are taking it very seriously. If the husband is to be arrested *and* the mother, what about the child?

(*Source:* Lilli Ngoyi, Leader A.N.C. on the Pass Campaign, 1956)

Protest again:

In March 1960 the Pan-African Congress (see page 58) called for a massive day of protest against the pass laws. People were urged to leave their passes at home and invite arrest – thus causing chaos to the system. In many areas of South Africa the protest began on Monday, 21 March. In the town of Sharpeville (the African township of Vereeniging), a large crowd of men, women and children converged on the police station, mostly to witness the protest and to hear an announcement which rumour had suggested was about to be made.

At 1.40 p.m. the police opened fire with sub-machine guns and pistols, firing about 700 rounds into the crowd. Sixty-nine Africans were killed and 160 wounded.

There were hundreds of women, some of them laughing. They must have thought the police were firing blanks. One woman was hit about ten yards from our car. Her companion, a young man, went back when she fell. He thought she had stumbled. Then he turned her over and saw her chest had been shot away. . . . One little boy had an old black coat which he held up behind his head, thinking perhaps, that it might save him from the bullets. Some of the children, hardly as tall as the grass, were leaping like rabbits. Some of them were shot too.

(*Source:* Humphrey Tyler (a white South African), Assistant Editor of *Drum*. Account published in the *Observer*, 27 March 1960)

South African police firing on unarmed protesters was not a new experience (see page 34, and there were many other instances besides these). What made Sharpeville different was that it became a symbol for people, both in South Africa and all over the world, who rejected the logic and legitimacy of Apartheid as a political system. Sharpeville was also the outcome of a growing impatience among the non-white communities with the tactics of protest represented by the determined non-violence of the Congresses. The protest at Sharpeville was itself non-violent (as all the pass law demonstrations were to be), but the violence with which it was met broke the patience of the protesters. For the government, Sharpeville helped towards the fulfilment of the long-held Afrikaner dream of an independent republic. All ties with Britain were to be broken. Now it was possible to introduce immensely harsh laws with which to crush opposition to Apartheid.

The outcomes of protest in the 1950s, culminating in Sharpeville, will be looked at in the next chapter.

Try to find out more about the Defiance Campaign organized by the A.N.C. in 1952-3.

ON REFLECTION:

Why do you think the Freedom Charter was ignored by the government?

The Armed Struggle: 1960-84

APARTHEID TRIUMPHANT? 1960-74

Throughout its existence, South Africa had had close constitutional links with the United Kingdom, first as a colony, then as a dominion within the Empire and Commonwealth. The head of state of South Africa was the British monarch. For many Afrikaners, this situation perpetuated the humiliation of their defeat in the Boer War. Their dream was a South Africa independent and separate.

On 31 May 1961 South Africa became a republic outside the Commonwealth. The Afrikaners' dream had come true. The date was the anniversary of the Peace of Vereeniging that had ended the Boer War.

Prime Minister Verwoerd had announced his intention of holding a referendum (among white voters) on whether South Africa should become a republic, early in 1960. It was something of a gamble. There was still a commitment to the British monarchy, and certainly one to the Commonwealth, not only among Anglo-Saxon whites, but also among some moderate Afrikaners, of whom Jan Smuts had once been the chief representative. In an attempt to secure a majority, Verwoerd promised to seek to remain a member of the Commonwealth, as India had done, despite its republican status.

Between January 1960 and March 1961 two events helped to make the gamble pay off. In February 1960, Harold Macmillan, the British Prime Minister, on a visit to South Africa, warned the South African government and the whites that they would continue to ignore black aspirations at their peril and that Britain could not support the policy of Apartheid. Then, in March, came the massacres at Sharpeville, Langa and elsewhere. Nationalist politicians were quick to blame the disturbances on Macmillan's speech, accusing him of giving blacks ideas above their station and of playing into the hands of the communists whom the Nationalists regarded as inspiring all "native" unrest.

In October 1960 Verwoerd won a majority for the republic in the referendum, and in March 1961 he flew to London for the Commonwealth Prime Ministers' Conference. Verwoerd's description of Apartheid as a policy of "good neighbourliness" did little to impress the Commonwealth Prime Ministers, with Sharpeville and their people's reaction to it so clearly in their minds. India and Ghana wanted South Africa out of the Commonwealth; Canada supported them. Compromise was impossible and on 15 March Verwoerd withdrew his application for membership.

Reaction at home:

We have been thrown out of the Commonwealth, put out of the group of the most tolerant, the most civilised, the most fair-minded people in the world. And we have been thrown out because of the narrow-minded inflexible doctrines of racism which began the sabotage of South Africa in 1948 and came to their climax under the direction of Dr Verwoerd.

(*Source: The Cape Times*, March 1961)

A Republic within the Commonwealth would have been a regrettable compromise, accepted only in the interests of white unity and because it would be preferable to no republic at all. It would never have had the same emotional appeal as a republic that had broken all constitutional ties with the historic enemy. Verwoerd had now achieved the historic ideal. . .

(*Source:* Henry Kenney, *Architect of Apartheid*, biography of Verwoerd, 1975)

Which of these views do you think represents which group of white South Africans?

In what sense was the republic a fulfilment of the Afrikaner dream?

How do you think black South Africans may have felt about this?

ECONOMIC TRIUMPH

The underlying impetus that produced and perpetuated Apartheid (and the forms of segregation that preceded it) has been the determination of the white minority, and particularly of the less well-off Afrikaner whites, to seize and secure wealth, income and ownership in their own hands.

The Native Land Acts, the civilized labour policies of the pre-Apartheid governments, and the whole structure of Apartheid itself were designed to secure this end.

BLACK LABOUR

It is accepted Government policy that the Bantu are only temporarily resident in the European areas of the Republic, for as long as they offer their labour there. As soon as they become, for some reason or another, no longer fit for work or superfluous in the labour market, they are expected to return to their country of origin or the territory of the national unit where they fit in ethnically if they were not born and bred in the homeland.

(*Source:* The Secretary for Bantu Administration, General Circular No 25, 1967)

Estimated *per capita* income, 1962-3:

Whites £624: non-whites under £37 [per year]
Average starting cash wages per month for African men in Johannesburg: £16.2s.6d
In the mines, average wage for 1963: Whites £1,281 p.a.; Coloureds and Asians £229; Africans £76 (in addition, compound accommodation and native food)

(*Source:* from *A Survey of Race Relations in South Africa*, 1964)

The pass laws, the policy of keeping Africans in, or sending them back to, bantustans or homelands, lack of political rights, illegality of trade unions, Bantu education. Explain how each of these policies helps keep black South Africans at the bottom of the economic ladder.

BEATING THE ENGLISH AT THEIR OWN GAME

Throughout South Africa's history the "commanding heights" of the economy – mining, manufacturing, banking and finance – had been the preserve of English-speaking whites. As a result, the really rich and economically powerful people in South African society were English. Afrikaner nationalism was not content for Afrikaners to be second-class citizens to the Anglo-Saxon whites.

At the time of the Sharpeville massacre, world reaction to the growing tension in South Africa had caused a massive crisis in the South African economy as foreign investors withdrew their funds. But, before long, these funds were flowing back into the country and the kind of person who benefited most was the new breed of Afrikaner capitalist.

Afrikaners in business:

A leader in the new Afrikaner business field of the time described the requirements for the true *entrepreneur*. He should be a creator, he said, whose creative deeds are in the service of the community. . . . He should . . . apply his talents so that by means of increased opportunities for employment his fellow Afrikaners would find a meaningful place for themselves in their own country. In all, enterprises should be strictly built on sound economic principles, but consistently provide increased opportunities for eager young Afrikaners to enter the world of business.

(*Source:* An account of M.S. Louw's article in *Tegniek*, June 1965, given in the *The Puritans in Africa*, W.A. de Klerk, London, 1975)

Housing for European employers of an industrial concern in the Transvaal, 1950.

By the end of the 1960s the spectre of Afrikaner urban poverty seemed to have melted away.

BREAKING THE OPPOSITION

Government "toleration" of African political organizations came to an end after Sharpeville. Up until then, although individuals had been harassed and arrested, banned and imprisoned, the bare right of political organization had been recognized. After Sharpeville, this right was removed and a series of acts were passed which allowed the State Police virtually unlimited powers in dealing with protesters.

On 18 April 1960 the A.N.C. and P.A.C. were declared banned organizations. Thousands of people were arrested and imprisoned without trial, under the State of Emergency that had been introduced following the Sharpeville massacre.

Deciding that it was hopeless to attempt to change the policies of the Nationalist government through peaceful opposition, the African National Congress announced its intention of continuing in existence as an underground organization. It abandoned its policy of non-violence and formed a military wing whose job it would be to train supporters to commit acts of sabotage against government installations. *Umkhonto We Sizwe* (The Spear of the Nation) was launched on 16 December 1961 when a series of attacks blew up pylons and municipal offices in Johannesburg and Port Elizabeth.

Abandoning non-violence:

It is . . . well known that the main national liberation organisations in this country have consistently followed a policy of non-violence. They have conducted themselves peaceably at all times, regardless of government attacks and persecutions upon them, and despite all government-inspired attempts to provoke them to violence. They have done so because the people prefer peaceful methods of change to achieve their aspirations without the suffering and bitterness of civil war. But the people's patience is not endless.

The time comes in the life of any nation when there remain only two choices: submit or fight. That time has now come to South Africa. We shall not submit and we have no choice but to hit back by all means within our power in defence of our people, our future and our freedom.

(*Source:* statement of Umkhonto, issued 16 December 1961)

What argument does Umkhonto use to justify the resort to violence?

Given what you have read, do you think their argument is valid?

THE GOVERNMENT'S RESPONSE

Through the rest of the 1960s increasingly severe laws were passed to suppress and contain the opposition movements. The police were empowered to arrest and imprison anyone without having to give any reason or show any cause.

1961: 12-day detention without trial
1963: 90-day detention without trial
1965: 180-day detention without trial
1966: 14-day renewable detention
1967: Indefinite detention for interrogation of suspected terrorists

Detainees could be held in solitary confinement, and there was no legal requirement to inform their family, lawyer or doctor of their detention. People could simply disappear, as there was no official method of obtaining information about anyone held under these laws.

The detention laws in practice:

Sun Chetty was defence lawyer for many black clients. He fled the country in 1978 and in exile spoke about the police methods:

You simply hold a detainee in solitary confinement until he breaks. The kind of people who may be involved with some sort of political organisation are usually outgoing, extrovert types who need other human beings. With no human contact, nothing to read, few clothes, they break sooner or later.

There may be some assault. . . . Keep them awake. Use the imaginary chair. Make the detainee sit against the wall on an imaginary chair . . . hold a sharp point under your chin so that if you sink towards the floor it sticks in your throat. . .

Every detainee I have ever represented has always been broken by this sort of treatment. No one can hold out. In the end you tell them everything. You even make it up. It all comes out. Fifty, sixty pages of confession. I have known as many as a hundred and twenty pages. You tell them everything about yourself and your friends.

(*Source:* Quoted in *The White Tribe of Africa,* D. Harrison, BBC Publications, 1981)

Find out what Habeas Corpus is and what part it plays in English law.

For which I am prepared to die:

In 1964, at the trial of Nelson Mandela and other A.N.C. leaders who had helped form Umkhonto We Sizwe, Mandela explained to the court what black South Africans were fighting for:

Africans want to be paid a living wage. Africans want to perform work which they are capable of doing, and not work which the government declares them to be capable of. Africans want to live where they obtain work. . . . Africans want to own land in places where they work. . . . African men want to have their wives and children to live with them where they work. . . . African women want to be with their menfolk and not left permanently widowed in the reserves. . . . We want to travel in our own country. . . . We want a just share in the whole of South Africa. . .

Above all, we want equal political rights. . .

During my lifetime I have dedicated myself to this struggle of the African people. . . . I have cherished the ideal of a democratic and free society in which all persons live together in harmony. . . . It is an ideal which I hope to live for and achieve. But if needs be it is an ideal for which I am prepared to die.

(*Source:* Nelson Mandela, address to court, May 1964, quoted in *Nelson Mandela* by Mary Benson, Penguin, 1986)

Mandela and his friends were imprisoned for life.

Imagine you are a white supporter of the government. Explain to a white liberal friend, who has been moved and impressed by Mandela's speech, why you think it is of no account.

By 1970 the opposition groups in South Africa were effectively crushed. The leaders were either in prison or in exile. South Africa's economy was booming and, as a result, many blacks living in the towns were enjoying a higher standard of living. Economic success, from which all the whites benefited, and the threat of armed black resistance from the the A.N.C. meant that many English-speaking whites now supported Nationalist policies of Apartheid. The repressive laws of the government were successfuly controlling what opposition seemed to continue to exist. For the whites in their beautiful suburbs, enjoying the highest standard of living in the world, Apartheid had fulfilled its promises of wealth and security.

The trouble for them was that the blacks in the townships, on whose behalf Mandela had spoken, did not see it in quite the same way.

THE LAAGER BESIEGED

The history of South Africa from 1974 to the present day is one of continuing and deepening crisis. The economic boom came to an end as the world price of oil rose. South Africa had undertaken massive spending on armaments, in order to threaten newly independent black states around its borders, pursue the war in Namibia and Angola, and suppress dissent in the townships. Now this spending was putting a severe strain on industry. All this, together with persistent inflation, threatened the economic success of Apartheid. The demands of Afrikaner business put at risk the unity of Nationalism, by opening up the age-old divisions between the *verligte* (pragmatic) and *verkrampte* (conservative) Nationalists. And, in particular, black protest re-emerged in the 1970s, as the most potent threat of all.

BLACK PROTEST

The Black Consciousness Movement among black intellectual youth began the process of reasserting the rights of blacks and regenerating their sense of dignity. The movement also began to rebuild the unity of the non-white populations, as coloured and Indian young people learnt from the new ideas. Because industry needed labour, and because many blacks persistently refused to submit passively to starvation in the "homelands", the black townships began to burst at the seams with "unofficial" black residents. Inflation and growing unemployment helped develop the protest. Black anger started to boil over and increasingly, since 1976, white policy in South Africa has been a series of acts designed to appease, contain or suppress it. Since 1976 the history of black South Africans has been a history of action: the history of white South Africans one of reaction.

If we die, so what? So long as liberation is gained.

(*Source:* a South African school student, interviewed for British television, 1986)

SOWETO: 1976

In 1976 the government announced that half of all subjects taught in schools were to be taught in Afrikaans. Schools in the black townships were already in a state of crisis – overcrowded, under-staffed, short of books (in any language) and equipment. In Soweto they were having to operate a shift system in order to try to fit everyone in. To the students, the Afrikaans order was the last straw.

On 16 June 1976 the Soweto school students staged a massive demonstration against the new orders. Police entered the township and dispersed the students, using tear-gas and bullets. Hector Peterson, aged thirteen, was the first child to die.

In memory of hector peterson:

i wish i loved
this my master's language
then perhaps
hector would be alive
but then
    i do not
i wish i could speak
this my master's language
then perhaps
a mother would know no sorrow
but then
    i cannot
for where the blood was spilled
there a sapling grew
of hatred
    mistrust
        revenge
nurtured and nourished
by the tears of all that grieved
and it is under the shadow
cold
of this tree
that all africa shall be
until a mother know peace.

(*Source:* "In memory of hector peterson", Mogorosi Motshumi)

No one knows how many children died in Soweto on that day. The police told reporters that it was none of their business when they attempted to count the piled-up bodies.

Protests spread across South Africa. Schools were boycotted, government offices attacked. In the next four months government figures record 500 blacks killed by police, although the figure is probably higher. Many thousands more were injured. Thousands disappeared into detention. Two white people had died on the first day of the protests in Soweto.

Make a list of the things that you would like to see changed in your school. Then think of all the different ways you might set about changing them. Are any of the things wrong with your school important enough to risk your life to change? Why do you think South African black school children are prepared to risk their lives?

THE RESULTS OF BANTU EDUCATION IN THE 1980s

What did you learn in school today, dear little child of mine?
What did you learn in school today, dear little child of mine?
We learnt that west is always best and white is usually right
That rich and poor will always be, and that's what makes us free.

What did you learn in school today, dear little child of mine?
What did you learn in school today, dear little child of mine?
That education brings opportunities in this advancing age
But we'll end up working in the factories for a measly weekly wage.

What did you learn on the streets today, dear little child of mine?
What did you learn on the streets today, dear little child of mine?
We learnt that teargas burns the eyes, we learnt how police dogs bite
We learnt that batons break our bones, and we're learning how to fight.

What did you hear in the news today, dear little child of mine?
What did you hear in the news today, dear little child of mine?
That agitators stir us up – and lead us all astray
But we can think and we can see and we want change today.

(*Source:* Cape Town school students' song)

To what extent does this song show that the protests of school students have now gone beyond protesting against the conditions in schools?

ADAPT OR DIE

In 1979 the Nationalist Party elected a new Prime Minister, P.W. Botha, whose slogan became "adapt or die". Industry needed a stable, skilled workforce with which it could negotiate (for strikes among African workers had been increasingly disruptive of industry throughout the 1970s). Secondly, the armed forces, who were becoming more and more powerful in South Africa since the independence, under black governments, of neighbouring states, needed a reliable black recruiting base. Sensitive to these demands, the Prime Minister instituted a series of measures which attempted to break up the united opposition to Apartheid among the non-white community. In an attempt to curtail their growing authority, black trade unions were invited to take part in the official negotiating systems established by the government. The presence of certain groups of blacks in the townships was recognized as permanent, and government-appointed town councils were created to run the townships. Constitutional changes were proposed which would create a parliament with three houses, one for whites, one for Indians and one for coloureds.

The new constitution:

. . . the 1983 Constitution Bill [proposed] a three-chamber parliament with 45 seats for an Indian chamber, 85 for 'coloureds' and 178 for whites. The three chambers elected members to an electoral college on the same 4:2:1 ratio so that it comprised 50 whites, 25 'coloureds' and 13 'Indians'. In September 1984 this college elected Mr P.W. Botha as executive president with near-dictatorial powers. He is serving a seven year term and successful impeachment is extremely difficult. A

Hector Peterson was the first child to die in Soweto.

President's Council of 60 members, 25 nominated by the President, the rest elected on the 4:2:1 ratio, discuss affairs defined by the President as 'common to all racial groups'.

(*Source: South Africa in the 1980s*, Catholic Institute of International Relations, 3rd edition, 1986)

Think out what your response to these proposals would be if you were (a) a supporter of the A.N.C.; (b) a conservative Afrikaner white.

THE UNITED DEMOCRATIC FRONT

At the elections to the tri-cameral (three-chamber) parliament in August 1984, only 16% of those Indians and "coloureds" eligible registered their vote. The success of this boycott was a result of the campaigning of the newly formed United Democratic Front.

Helen Joseph speaking at the launch of the U.D.F. She had led many of the protests against Apartheid in the 1950s and was one of the treason trial defendants with Nelson Mandela.

The U.D.F. is an umbrella organization consisting of some 650 groups, including Christian and Islamic groups, women's and students' organizations, sporting and cultural groups. It represents the success of the black communities in building unity among many of the people, white and non-white, who are opposed to Apartheid. This has been achieved, despite the government's efforts to divide the non-white communities by providing economic benefits for some and political benefits for others. The U.D.F. also represents the coming together of three strands of political thinking among the black communities: the pride in self, race and community of the Black Consciousness Movement; the socialist and Utopian tradition of the Freedom Charter; and the original call for unity that Seme issued when he founded the A.N.C. in 1911 (see page 31).

Beginning in 1984, many members have been imprisoned, detained and banned. Since 1984 over half of the U.D.F. office holders have been arrested, charged with high treason or murdered.

Epilogue: South Africa since 1984

In September 1984 the black townships of the Vaal triangle staged a protest against rent increases. One township was surrounded by 7,000 troops. Since that day the black townships of South Africa have been under almost permanent occupation, and over 2,000 black residents have died.

Troops in the township of Tsakawe, East Rand, 1985.

31 January 1985: President Botha to the South African Assembly:

The Government is willing to consider Mr Mandela's release in the Republic of South Africa on condition that Mr Mandela gives a commitment that he will not make himself guilty of planning, instigating or committing acts of violence for the furtherance of political objectives. . . . It is therefore not the South African government which now stands in the way of Mr Mandela's freedom. It is he himself. The choice is his. All that is required of him now is that he should unconditionally reject violence as a political instrument. . .

10 February 1985: U.D.F. meeting at Soweto: Nelson Mandela's reply read to the people by Zindzi Mandela:

. . . I am surprised at the conditions that the government wants to impose on me. I am not a violent man. . . . It was only when all other forms of resistance were no longer open to us, that we turned to the armed struggle. Let Botha . . . renounce violence. . . . Let him guarantee free political activity so that the people may decide who will govern them.

I cherish my own freedom dearly, but I care even more for your freedom. Too many have died since I went to prison. Too many have suffered for the love of freedom. I owe it to their widows, to their orphans, to their mothers and to their fathers who have grieved and wept for them.

Not only I have suffered during these long, lonely, wasted years. I am not less life-loving than you are. But I cannot sell my birthright, nor am I prepared to sell the birthright of the people to be free. . .

Only free men can negotiate. Prisoners cannot enter into contracts. . .

I cannot and I will not give any undertaking at a time when I and you, the people, are not free. . .

Despite the presence of armed troops and police in the townships, the struggle continued. Attacks on government offices and personnel increased. The continuing evidence that the government was under siege and unable to reassert its power, as it had done in 1961, led to a major economic crisis in August 1985 when South Africa found itself unable to pay foreign debts that had fallen due. A State of Emergency, giving wide-ranging powers to the armed forces and the police, was declared in selected districts in June 1985. Internationally, the call for economic sanctions, the release of Nelson Mandela and the legalization of the A.N.C. became more pressing.

In the first half of 1986 a group of leading statesmen of the Commonwealth went to South Africa to investigate the possibilities of encouraging the South African government to change its policies and re-establish peace. Leaders of the U.D.F. met this group and clearly outlined their position:

A fundamental transformation of this society:

The UDF wish to emphasise that we are not waging a civil rights struggle – a struggle for reforms. We are resisting the very basis of economic exploitation and political domination in our land. In our view the democratisation of the South African State can only be effected by a fundamental transformation of this society – a transformation which our rulers cannot countenance.

We know that we have no option but to intensify our struggle at all levels. We expect a concomitant increase in state terror. . .

There is still time for the racist minority regime to consult the authentic leaders of the people with the sole objective of making the necessary arrangements for the speedy and effective dismantling of the apartheid state and transfer of power to the people. . .

While the UDF is not opposed to a negotiated transfer of power, bitter experience makes it sceptical of any attempts to persuade the Botha regime to negotiate at this stage.

(*Source:* from Memo of the National Executive Committee of the U.D.F., April 1986)

In June 1986 the State of Emergency was extended to the whole country and has been in force ever since. Controls amounting to censorship were placed on the media at that time and were tightened further in November 1986.

ON REFLECTION:

What do you think are the prospects for peaceful change in South Africa?

Glossary

Afrikaans the language spoken by the descendants of the Dutch settlers in South Africa

Afrikaners the descendants of the Dutch settlers in South Africa. They make up about 60% of the white population

ama-Zulu Zulu nation or Zulu people

A.N.C. African National Congress: founded in 1912 and recognized by most people as the political representative of the South African people of African descent

Apartheid an Afrikaans word meaning apartness: the philosophical, legal and political system by which the white communities in South Africa control the non-white communities

bang or bhang: Indian hemp, the leaves of which, when smoked, have narcotic and intoxicating properties

Bantu 1. the term used by linguists to identify the family of languages spoken by many people in sub-Saharan Africa
2. the term used by the Nationalist government after 1948, to describe South Africans of African descent; it has become closely identified with the ideology of Apartheid

bantustans the term used by the South African government, after 1948, to describe the reserves established under the Native Land Acts of 1913 and 1936

Barolong a sub-group of the Tswana people

Basuto really Ba-sotho: the Sotho people

B.C.M. Black Consciousness Movement, which developed in the 1970s

Black 1. the official Apartheid term for South Africans of African descent; adopted after the protests against Bantu education and Bantu Administration Boards, 1976 onwards
2. term used by opponents of Apartheid to describe all non-white South Africans (used since the 1970s and the growth of black consciousness)

black spot areas of land occupied or owned by Africans (usually surrounded by white-owned land) and which the government has designated for use by another group (usually white). Occupants of black spots are forcibly removed to the bantustans

Boer an Afrikaans word meaning farmer: now an old-fashioned word for Afrikaners

Bushmen the term used by white people to describe the San people

Caffres *see* Kafirs

client community a group of people dependent on another for their survival, e.g. through food, protection

coloured the term used to describe several groups of people: in terms of Apartheid classification, it includes all those of "mixed race" descent, descendants of the Malay slaves brought to the Cape in the eighteenth century, and of the Khoi-Khoi and the San peoples

Congress of Democrats a left-wing white anti-Apartheid organization founded in 1952; participated in the Congress of the People 1954; banned 1962

dompas *see* pass

endorsed out expelled from an urban area if not entitled to be there under the pass laws; the pass book is endorsed to that effect

Fingoes *see* Mfengu

homelands *see* bantustans

Hottentots the term used by many white people to describe the Khoi-Khoi people

influx control the system which prevents people who live in the bantustans from moving to, living and working in the urban areas. The pass laws are used to effect this

Kafirs from the Arabic, meaning heathen or unbeliever; the term used by many Afrikaners to describe all South Africans of African descent, but originally applied to the Xhosa people

Khoi-Khoi one of the earliest peoples inhabiting the southern peninsula of Africa. They kept cattle. They were one of the first groups to have contact with white sailors and settlers

laager the defensive ring made from ox-wagons used by the people on the Great Trek

Mfengu refugees from the Mfecane who crossed into Transkei and re-established an identity for themselves

Nguni people whose language belongs to the Bantu family who moved furthest to the south-east during the southern expansion fo the Bantu-speakers; including the Zulu, the Mthethwa and the Xhosa peoples

P.A.C. Pan-African Congress. A group which broke away from the A.N.C. in 1959, considering it to be too moderate and too tolerant of other non-African groupings in South Africa. It believes that South Africa, its land and resources should belong only to people of African descent

pass the certificate which all Africans have to carry to establish their right to be in a particular area. In April 1986 the government announced its intention of abolishing the pass law system, but not to yield control of movements of African people

Pedi the people who lived in what is now North East Transvaal; defeated and annexed by the white settlers in 1879

Rand (R) 1. the South African unit of currency.
2. the area south of Johannesburg where gold is mined

reserves *see* bantustans

San people who were among the earliest inhabitants of the southern peninsula of Africa. They were hunter-gatherers: called "bushmen" by the whites

Sotho group of people, whose language belongs to the Bantu family, living west of the Drakensburg mountains. Under their king Moshoeshoe, they succeeded in surviving the Mfecane and formed the Lesotho state (called formerly by the whites Basutoland). It preserves a fragile independence which still exists today, though economically it is effectively a client state of South Africa

Tswana the group of peoples living in the north-western area of what is now the Transvaal, the Orange Free State, the Northern Cape and the independent state of Botswana. The southern Tswana lived in the area where diamonds were found, but were moved out. In the bantustan system of South Africa they are confined to the homeland of Bophuthatswana, a small area in the northern Cape on the Botswana border

U.D.F. United Democratic Front

Xhosa The southernmost Nguni, who had the greatest contact from earliest on with the white settlers. They fought a number of wars against territorial encroachment by the whites, but were finally defeated

Sources and Book List

These are combined as there are very few easily available unpublished sources on South Africa. The following list is highly selective: there are many other books which will find referred to in the bibliographies of those mentioned here.

EARLY EXPLORERS AND INVESTIGATORS

ed. D. Moodie: *The Record . . . of the Native Tribes of South Africa: extracts from van Riebeeck's Journal* (Amsterdam, 1960)
A.T. Bryant: *Olden Times in Zululand and Natal* (London, 1920)
H.F. Fynn: *The Diary of Henry Francis Fynn* (Pietermaritzburg, 1950)

BIOGRAPHIES AND AUTOBIOGRAPHIES

K. Hancock: *The Sanguine Years* and *The Fields of Force* (Biography of Jan Smuts) (Cambridge University Press, 1962 and 1968)
H. Kenney: *Architect of Apartheid* (biography of Verwoerd) (Johannesburg, 1975)
W. Mandela: *Part of My Soul* (autobiography) (Penguin, 1985)

AFRIKANER HISTORY

D. Harrison: *The White Tribe of Africa* (BBC Publications, 1981)
W.A. de Klerk: *The Puritans in Africa* (London, 1975)
F.A. van Jaarsveld: *From Van Riebeeck to Vorster 1652-1974* (Perskor Publishers, 1975)

BLACK HISTORY

E. Roux: *Time Longer than Rope* (University of Wisconsin Press, 1964)
M. Benson: *South Africa. The Struggle for a Birthright* (history of the ANC) (Penguin, 1966)
H.J. and R.E. Simons: *Class and Colour in South Africa* (London, 1969)

GENERAL HISTORIES

D. Denoon: *South Africa since 1800* (Longman, 1972)
C.W. de Kieweit: *A History of South Africa: Social and Economic* (Oxford, 1941)
G.H.L. LeMay: *Black and White in South Africa* (London, 1971)

CONTEMPORARY WITNESSES

A. Lutuli: *Let My People Go* (London, 1962)
N. Mandela: *No Easy Walk to Freedom* (London, 1965)
T. Huddleston: *Naught For Your Comfort* (Collins, 1956)

OTHER BOOKS AND SOURCES

It is a good idea to read the work of South African novelists, both black and white, such as Olive Schreiner, Alan Paton, Ezekial Mphahlele. There are plays and poems too, all of which help to give a more intimate idea of life in South Africa. The British Defence and Aid Fund for Southern Africa has helped in the production of a number of resources on contemporary issues. A list of their resources can be obtained from BDAF, 64 Essex Road, London N1 8LR.

Timeline

Notes: **c**: (circa) around about that time **BC**: Before Christ

PERIOD	DATES	SIGNIFICANT EVENTS IN BRITAIN	SIGNIFICANT WORLD EVENTS
Pre-Industrial South Africa	**up to 1867**	**1793-1815** French Revolutionary and Napoleonic Wars **1807** Slave trade abolished **1832** Great Reform Act **1834** Emancipation of slaves in British colonies **1867** Second Reform Act	**1480s** Start of Portuguese period of exploration **1595** Dutch claim Java, Borneo and rest of Dutch East Indies **1793** Holland occupied by France **1802-3** Peace of Amiens; lull in the French Revolutionary and Napoleonic Wars **1861-65** American Civil War **1863** American emancipation of slaves
South Africa: Mineral Revolution to Union	**1867-1910**	**1875** Britain buys the Suez Canal **1876** Queen Victoria proclaimed "Empress of India" **1884** Third Reform Act: virtually all men over the age of 21 now have the vote **1884-5** Conference of Berlin: agreed division of Africa between European powers **1906** Election of Liberal government; reforming ministry	**1884-5** Berlin Conference: 15 nations meet to divide Central Africa
Union to Nationalist Victory	**1910-48**	**1914-18** First World War **1926** General Strike **1931** Statute of Westminster: basis of modern Commonwealth **1935** India Act: giving increased representation to Indians in the election of Indian government **1939-45** Second World War **1945** Election of majority Labour government **1947** India granted independence	**1914-18** First World War **1919** Treaty of Versailles **1935** Italy invades Ethiopia **1939-45** Second World War **1945** Creation of the United Nations **1946** India terminates trade and diplomatic relations with South Africa

AD: (Anno Domini) In the Year of Our Lord   **Century:** a hundred years

SIGNIFICANT EVENTS IN AFRICA	SIGNIFICANT EVENTS IN SOUTH AFRICA
10th century on Development of major states in West Africa Zenith of Zimbabwe **1450 on** Development of West African trade with Portugal **1562** West African nations commence slave trade with Britain **1575** Portugal claims sovereignty over Angola and Mozambique **1800 on** Europeans extend their explorations inland	**1000 on** Sotho and Nguni states well-established in central plateau and eastern seaboard **1486** Khoi-Khoi have first contact with Portuguese explorers **1497** Nguni have first contact with Portuguese explorers **1652** Dutch settlement at Cape **1779** First Xhosa War **1780** Great Fish River claimed by Dutch as eastern boundary of colony **1795** British occupy Cape **1806** Reoccupation of Cape by British **1828** Citizenship granted to "all free persons of colour" in Cape Death of Shaka **1834** Emancipation of slaves at Cape **1836** Great Trek **1838** Battle of Blood River: Zulus defeated by Trekkers and African allies **1860** First Indian indentured labour brought to Natal
1869 Suez Canal opens **1885-1900** Partition of Africa: domination of European states **1895** Defeat of Ashanti Empire in West Africa by British **1903** Britain defeats North Nigerian kingdoms	**1867** Diamonds discovered **1880** First Boer War **1881** British defeated at Majuba Hill: Transvaal returned to Boers **1886** Gold discovered in the Rand **1887** Annexation of Zululand by British **1894** Glen Grey Act **1899-1902** Second Boer War **1906** Indian Pass Law in Natal **1910** Union of four Crown Colonies to form Union of South Africa
1914-18 Annexation of German colonies by France and Britain **1919** Treaty of Versailles: ex-German colonies become mandated territories of League of Nations; administered by Britain and France **1924** Indian community in Kenya given representation on Legislative Council **1936** Ethiopia annexed by Italy after bitter war **1939-45** Second World War **1947** Degree of self-government won in Nigeria	**1912** A.N.C. founded **1913** Native Land Act **1919** A.N.C. pass burning campaign I.C.U. founded **1920** African miners' strike **1922** White miners' strike: Rand revolt **1925** The Wage Act **1926** Colour Bar Act **1927** Hostility Act First African trades unions founded in Rand **1936** Native Representation and Land Acts **1938** Voortrekker Centenary celebrations **1943** First Alexandra bus strike **1946** Great African miners' strike: many killed and injured and leaders arrested **1948** Election of Nationalist government Implementation of Apartheid

Timeline

Notes: **c: (circa)** around about that time **BC:** Before Christ

PERIOD	DATES	SIGNIFICANT EVENTS IN BRITAIN	SIGNIFICANT WORLD EVENTS
Nationalist Victory to Sharpeville	**1948-60**	**1956** Invasion of Suez **1957 on** Britain grants independence to African colonies	**1952** U.N. General Assembly begins series of debates on the broader questions of Apartheid
Sharpeville to the present day	**1960-86**	**1964** Labour government bans arms sales to South Africa **1965** Britain seeks U.N. help over Rhodesian rebellion **1970** M.C.C. cuts off cricketing links with South Africa **1980** Rhodesian independence negotiated	**1960** Security Council of the U.N. calls on South Africa to end Apartheid **1961** Commonwealth rejects South Africa's application for membership **1963** Voluntary arms embargo instituted by Security Council United States institutes partial arms embargo **1977** Security Council unanimously imposes a mandatory arms embargo **1986** United States, Britain, the E.E.C. and the Commonwealth implement varying degrees of economic sanctions against South Africa

AD: (Anno Domini) In the Year of Our Lord **Century:** a hundred years

SIGNIFICANT EVENTS IN AFRICA	SIGNIFICANT EVENTS IN SOUTH AFRICA
1950 New constitutions for Gold Coast, Nigeria and Sierra Leone: large degree of self-government **1952** Mau Mau campaign for independence using violence, Kenya **1957** Gold Coast independence: dominion of Ghana **1958** Guinea becomes independent	**1950** Suppression of Communism Act: Registration Act aimed at classifying the population by colour and race **1952** Defiance Campaign **1953** Bantu Education Act **1955** Adoption of Freedom Charter **1956** Cape Coloured removed from voters roll Treason Trial commences **1959** P.A.C. formed **1960** Sharpeville and Langa massacres: A.N.C. and P.A.C. banned State of Emergency
1973 African (and Arab) states impose oil embargo on South Africa **1965** Rhodesia declares independence unilaterally **1975** Mozambique and Angola win independence **1980** Rhodesian rebellion ends: Rhodesia becomes independent under democratic constitution: renamed Zimbabwe	**1961** South Africa becomes a republic, outside the Commonwealth Last of Treason Trial defendants found not guilty Umkhonto We Sizwe founded **1962** Sabotage Act: sabotage becomes a capital offence; house arrest for banned persons **1963** 90-Day detention Rivonia Trial of Mandela and his friends begins **1964** Rivonia defendants sentenced to life imprisonment Transkei (Bantustan) given legislative assembly **1965** 180-day detention **1973** Wave of strikes by black workers **1974** Internal Security Act passed **1976** Soweto massacre: widespread uprisings **1977** Death of Steve Biko in police detention **1980** Launch of campaign to release Nelson Mandela Oil-refinery near Durban damaged in major A.N.C. guerilla attack **1981** 20th anniversary of Republic **1982** Security Laws strengthened: Defence Act allows massive increase of expenditure on police and armed forces **1983** U.D.F. formed Constitutional changes proposed **1984** New constitution implemented Widespread uprisings **1985** C.O.S.A.T.U. (Congress of South African Trade Unions) formed South African business leaders meet A.N.C. in Zambia **1986** Nationwide State of Emergency

Index